THE SPIRITUAL LIFE
by
Michael Featherstone. BA (Hons) Fine Art. 2016

THE SPIRITUAL LIFE

First Edition

Copyright Michael Featherstone 2016

This book is copyrighted under the Berne Convention. All rights reserved. No part of this book may be reproduced or utilised in any form by any means, electronic or mechanical, including photocopying and recording, or by any information, storage and retrieval system without permission in writing from the publisher. Except for the purpose of reviewing or criticism as permitted under the Copyright Act of 1956.

Printed by Create Space. An Amazon.Com Company.

CONTENTS.

The Spiritual Life	P1.
Beginnings	P2.
The Book	P4.
My Inspiration	P5.
Introduction	P5.
The Queen's 60th Jubilee	P7.
The Power of Thought	P8.
The Rose	P9.
Life's Events	P10.
Laughter	P12.
Help From Above	P13.
Good and Bad Influences	P14.
Love	P15.
In the Beginning	P16.
The Grandeur of the Universe	P17.
Seeking to Understand	P18.
Victims of Circumstance	P18.
Turning Points	P20.
Lift your Mind	P21.
Small Packages	P22.
The Work of the Spirit	P23.
The Christ Within	P24.
When things go wrong	P25.
Feelings	P27.
Sugar & Spice	P28.
Living in Harmony	P28.
The Spirit World	P29.
A Journey of Enlightenment	P29.
Changing our Affinity with the Spirit World	P31.
A World of Insights	P31.
The World of Spirit	P32.
Individuality	P34.
The Spiritual Realms	P35.
Conscience	P36.
The Spiritual Planes	P37.
The Higher Realms	P38.
The Darkness	P39.

Guidance	P39.
Universal Love	P41.
Accentuate the Positive	P41.
Their Own Little Worlds	P42.
Bringing Peace into your World	P43.
God Never Leaves You	P43.
The Higher Self	P44.
Judgement	P45.
The Living Dream The Astral	P45.
Making Progress	P46.
Faith	P48.
Gloom and Despondency	P48.
Black Dog	P49.
Kind Words	P50.
Silver Lining	P51.
The Ups And Downs of Life	P52.
Optimism	P53.
Somewhere Over the Rainbow	P53.
The ladder of spirituality	P54.
God Walks With Us	P55.
The Power of Love	P55.
A New Outlook	P56.
Christ's Laws	P56.
Reaching Out	P57.
Bright Angels	P57.
Kindness	P58.
Heaven on Earth	P60.
Injustice	P60.
Despair	P62.
Going Higher	P62.
God's Love	P63.
Think Positive	P64.
The World	P64.
The Will of God	P66.
Love is all Around	P66.
People	P67.
The Gift of Love	P69.
Looking Back	P69.
The Mind	P70.
Of Heavens and Hells	P72.

Love in the afterlife	*P73.*
Separation	*P75.*
The Greatest Power in the universe	*P75.*
Positive Thoughts	*P76.*
Look for the Master in all Things	*P77.*
Hopes and Dreams	*P78.*
The New Year	*P78.*
Jesus	*P80.*
Of Christianity	*P82.*
Of Other Lives	*P83.*
Love and Hate	*P84.*
The Poor	*P85.*
Looking Forward	*P85.*
Our Special Challenge	*P86.*
Cause & Effect	*P87.*
The Stream of Life	*P88.*
Sharing Knowledge	*P90.*
Opposite Points of View	*P91.*
The Making of a Soul	*P92.*
The Good and Beautiful	*P93.*
A Spiritual Quest	*P94.*
The Voice of Spirit	*P95.*
Value Each Passing Moment	*P96.*
Taking Stock	*P96.*
Different Pathways	*P98.*
Blood, Sweat and Tears	*P99.*
The Many Ways of Learning	*P100.*
The Future	*P101.*
The Guides	*P102.*
The Helpers	*P103.*
The Time is Now	*P104.*
Sleep	*P104.*
Thinking of God	*P104.*
The Universe & Mankind	*P105.*
The True Value of Life	*P107.*
We are Greater Beings than we Realise	*P109.*

THE SPIRITUAL LIFE.

By Michael Featherstone.

For many people in this modern world, life has no meaning; for them existence is empty, hollow and filled with pain: But there is far more to life than they realise. Like the song of the birds the soft and gentle voice of spirit often goes unnoticed; helping; guiding; informing and comforting each and every one of us. They are with us every day of our lives from the moment of birth, until we meet face to face once again, on the day that we return to our spiritual home.

I believe that the thoughts that follow have, to a greater or lesser extent, been given to me to share with those who will listen. I hope that you will find these ideas as interesting and inspiring as I do.

BEGINNINGS.
The notion of a heaven above brings to mind an imaginary world beyond the clouds. In reality when someone unexpectedly finds themselves out of the body he or she rarely wants to come back except for the pull of loved ones left behind, though sometimes not even then. They find that it is our world that is the insubstantial dream-like existence, a sort of digital cloud, a virtual reality. The Spirit world is hyper real, beautiful beyond words with a powerful effect on the emotions. It is familiar, it is full of life and it is home: Like radio and television signals it is everywhere and only a thought away.

I have spent over forty years reading, thinking about and experiencing some amazing evidence for a life after death and trying to reconcile it with the sceptical viewpoint. As a Television Engineer for 35 years I know that you just as you cannot find faults with belief you have to use a logical step by step approach to this highly complicated and fascinating subject. This journey is contained within my book 'The Living Dream' in which I try to show that amongst the apparently bizarre activities and beliefs of human beings there are mountains of real evidence that the mind never dies.
The realisation that thoughts can originate outside of one's own mind is deeply profound and I personally have had more than enough proof that <u>thoughts from the so-called dead do filter into the minds of all of us.</u>
The words in this book are intended to be thought provoking and encouraging. This material is selected from recordings of 'inspired' speaking, sometimes when I was alone and at others with friends: It is aimed at helping us through from day to day. Some of the content is very personal and referring to my, at times, 'glass half empty' outlook which I'm sure many people can relate to. Other material includes thoughts about the big questions that we would all like to

know more about. We are all adventurers and as visitors to this world we can experience many things that can't be understood in a world where there is no pain, death or separation.

Though our own divine self can be the source of great wisdom, if these really are individuals sending out thoughts to us, who and what are they. You can think of them as guardian angels; guides; old friends; helpers and loved ones: My impression is that they are in one sense ordinary people like you and I, some of whom have known us before we were born and perhaps for countless centuries. This of course makes them extra ordinary as they are no longer confined by the limitations of the human brain or outlook. Their experience and knowledge covers many lives and they follow our fortunes trying to inspire us to get the best out of our adventures on earth. They like us are individuals and yet all part of that one amazing being that we call God.

I hope you find the following words interesting and food for thought so please take that which commends itself to your reason and leave the rest.
                Michael Featherstone. BA (Hons) Fine Art.2016.

THE BOOK.

The book we have given you is of the greatest simplicity, the honest, straightforward and true. Never let it be said that we were ambiguous, that we made ammunition to spark off another argument, a difference of opinion. The facts are there for all to see and the history of your world proves this for there are many books which tell of the help of the angels; of the spirit friends; the deities; the Gods and demy Gods. But the picture in men's minds must be levelled, made plain and simple with no allegiance to greater powers other than God Himself: No stories of powers in heaven that try to shape and mould in the manner of a man for spirits are wiser than that. They come in the name of The Lord to do His bidding, to keep His house in order, to explain to thinking people what benefit there is in the lives they are leading and what drawbacks there are for those who follow a purely material pathway. Everything is mixed, a portion of this a portion of that and all these things help to put together a rich and invigorating experience, that which you call life. We cannot be forever changing the script however the script changes as we write it. We make our plans, we have our hopes and desires and from these thoughts, these desires, follow the course of human life; the interacting; being rebuffed; helping; supporting; antagonising and all the human emotions as each individual weaves his or her way through this process of living: This mind bending; mind changing; mind altering experience from which we gain wisdom and knowledge and understanding of what it is like to be an individual with our own choices, our own agendas and our own determination to make something of the world we live in: To shape it; to mould it; to experience it in all its glory and in all its forms never for one moment doubting that God is our saviour. He looks after us; He follows our fortunes; He creates for us a garden in which we might dwell. He comes to us in the night to comfort us and in the day to see that we are on our mettle;

that we have a growing awareness; a strong desire to succeed; to make things better; to understand them; to learn; to grow and even to fail: For the God of all is the God of life.
July 2016.

MY INSPIRATION
We cannot come to you in the day as easily as we can during the night so when you are at rest you are in essence being primed for those moments when you need the information. Then we can do our best to instil within you the ideas, the proposals and the thoughts which you are expressing now. I have my way of coming to you, others have theirs and when we are together we make a great team. But nothing is set in stone, nothing we ever say is pure, unadulterated or undistorted; always remember that. So when you are assessing your notes, take the spirit of what is given to you and analyse it by using your instinct and your judgement. Take from it what you can and leave the rest for this is how it must be with all inspiration.
March 2012.

INTRODUCTION.
From the ends of the earth people are crying out for knowledge that they might understand the reason for their lives; why they are as they are; how they came to be here, and what the end of their life will be. Love* tries to give them the answer within their own minds, through their own inner knowledge, speaking to them as a father, as a friend and as a guide. *(* I found the use of the word 'love' unexpected!)* But they understand not that what they are feeling and what they believe in their innermost selves is the truth for it contradicts that which their conscious mind tells them, that which the world tells them and that which the so-called experts tell them. And so what they know in their innermost selves must be spoken out loud that they might understand that the knowledge which they have is the truth, is reality, is the way forward and is the reason for their existence on earth. I come

to you trying to help those souls who cry out in the night, in fear, in loneliness and in terror that they might take hold of our words and draw comfort from them and in so doing change the course of their lives: Bringing into their own situation a breath of fresh air, a lightening of the mood, a happier frame of mind and with this they can change the whole atmosphere amongst the people with which they live. Because you see one word of comfort, one word of good cheer, one word of understanding, goes a very long way. To you my dear friend we entrust our thoughts hoping that you will deliver them as directly and as clearly as is possible. It has been given to you to fulfil our wishes, to help us in our quest and to express that which we feel is badly needed in the world of man. When you come over to our side you will see the pain and suffering which hides behind the mask of normality and also that everyday people in everyday situations are uncertain and traumatised and concerned that their lives are meaningless and wasted. They know that they have so much to offer that cannot be expressed and in this frame of mind they feel bitter, depressed and helpless. But if only they could see the positive, the riches of life, the fundamental truths that we are what we are; spiritual beings going through life on a great adventure; seeking knowledge and understanding; forming opinions; making decisions; failing and succeeding. And all of these very valuable things are given to us that we might learn; that we might understand; that we might grow in stature and be better people more able to help others in their pain and sorrow, and in *their* quest for knowledge and love and understanding.

It is a great time in the history of man when he has so much to offer, and yet he understands so little. He claims to be so enlightened but he knows nothing of the reason for his existence or of the fundamental rules of life in the spiritual which has a direct effect upon the practical; the day to day living that we all must experience. And if only he could see, as we can see, the reality of life in its purest form then he would not be so downcast and would be able to play his part more fully and more perfectly: He would be able to participate with a greater heart and with more happiness and fulfilment.

THE QUEEN'S 60TH JUBILEE.

Good evening. We are all here, joining in the merriment. The celebrations have gone well and we know that the kingdom is united. From here we see a very different picture to the things that you see. We see the mood and the character of the country, how people really see and think and feel. And we know that there is a coming together, an uplift from such a celebration though it must be said there are dissenters. In our world we are all as one; we join together in everything we do; one harmonious whole and we work at it until we get it right. We come to you in the day, we come to you in the evening and we follow our plans until they come to fruition. And anything that gets in our way is considered and understood until we can get round it. And so you see there is always planning going on, always help at hand; instruction; structure; levels of understanding and coming together as one to make the world a better place. For in your world there are many injustices, many things to see to, to put right and though we cannot and do not attempt to change the course of events we can bring to the situation a better result, more understanding from the recipient, more knowledge about one's self and fellow man so that the events themselves bring about a change in character, a change in understanding and an upliftment in the spiritual sense. And though we do not always comprehend the way people think we work with them, we try to make them see a little light a little reason. We try to help them consider points of view that they had never considered before to try to put them on the right path. All of these things we ourselves have learned through our various lives. We have taken note of the things that we have done, we have understood where we have gone wrong, and even have the privilege of understanding where others have gone wrong. Where we have been in conflict we see who was right and who was wrong and why. And so we have a deeper knowledge into the human psyche from this side of life because we can really see the thoughts and the feelings that people have. When eventually you come to us you will realise that your life was mapped out and we had a hand in it. We tried to help you through to get the best out of everything and you will be glad of all the things you have experienced and learned and struggled and come to terms with. We give you these words with our blessings. Good night and God bless. 4th June 2012.

THE POWER OF THOUGHT.
In your minds you have many hopes and wishes and fears too and we want you to set about putting them in order that you might anticipate only the best, that you might feel the purpose and the pleasant longing for all things spiritual. In your minds there is great power and great potential and yet you neglect to use that power; you anticipate only the bad and the negative. In our world thoughts take shape; we come to you on wings of thought, we drive our chariots by the power of thought, everything we do is moulded by thought and yet you in your world are inclined to let thoughts take care of themselves. It is a power that is there to be used, to shape and mould, to increase your potential, to direct your own body, your own wishes and your desires. In the world of man there is a tendency to follow the dictates of the material, to let the day rule your mind instead of letting your mind rule the day: To look on brighter and fairer thoughts which will permeate through your body, which will radiate to other people and bring an atmosphere which is uplifting and which is worthy of the spiritual. And these thoughts must be cultivated so that you have only good thoughts, pleasant thoughts and positive thoughts in anticipation of something

that you are building which is a power; a strength; a unity and an agreement to go forward together. And in that power to hold a reservoir for when things are not so good you can draw from it and make it yours. For there is strength in numbers and together you will succeed and with your friends in the world of spirit who send you their loving thoughts, and their power too, you will create a mighty force. The real world beckons; leave behind the world of shadow, the world of dreams, take hold of the reins and fly on the wings of love. These thoughts I give to you with my love and my best wishes. God bless. January 1995.

THE ROSE.

A rose in a garden smells so sweet because of its nature, it manifests in accordance with the laws of nature laid down before time began. The evidence is there for all to see, a clear statement written in the design of the rose. We come to you tonight in the hope that you can see written in our statements a positive message, something that you will take home with you, which will help create within your mind a new beginning, a seed that will grow, to give you strength when you need it. All around you there are signs written in love, evidence before your own eyes that God is: That He is just and loving. In the years to come you will ponder much on the meaning of His love in a world that seems so filled with darkness and yet I tell you that it is there for all to see. - The creation in which we all live, the caring and the tenderness which is shown to each one of us despite our troubled minds and throughout our adventures, is there if you will look deep within and admit to yourselves that you have been, and always will be, guided and protected so that through everything and in everything that you do His influence is there. I want you to see for yourselves that it is His love that has brought you together, His love that teaches you and through your inner minds helps you to walk through the circumstances the barriers and the hazards and into His light.

The evidence is there friends for all to see and yet they cannot see it. Their minds are so conditioned with things as they are, so full of the material, of mortal life and yet we see clearly as you cannot see, His love always working, always protecting, always guiding. Though you may think of us as your guides and protectors, though you may look up to us unworthy though we are, we all of us are centred around that great power which is of God. We take from Him and yet we give little in return. He is our guide and mentor, that all-embracing power which created the Universe and yet He is ever present in the lives of each one of us. And so when you see the rose remember His presence, remember how sweet it smells, remember that He created it and the beauty that it displays is just one of the varied manifestations of His love in our lives. There is about you a great light, despite your feelings of being unworthy, of emptiness, and there is within each of you a sign, a light, a covenant that is written deep within your heart that can never be erased. In His good time He will bring you forward to flower like the rose for all to see. It is with these words I leave you my good friends.

August 1994.

LIFE'S EVENTS.

In your circle tonight there are friends and helpers who seek to know more about you, who are learning from you, who are determined to bring something into your lives which they feel will be of benefit: Friends old and new coming to uplift you, to serve you and to share in this unique experience which is the coming together of many minds focussed for a short while on one purpose. And that purpose is to make you all aware of our presence, to teach you in the ways of the spiritual, to educate you that you might in turn teach others.- To help them in their difficulties, to see light in the gloom, to see purpose midst chaos and to return them to the path from which they have strayed. It is a pleasure and an honour to speak to you in this manner for it is not given to many to hear their voice once again in the world of man though it be not my natural voice but the voice of my friend. And I take the opportunity of thanking you all and of bringing my best wishes and the wishes of your friends for your success. In our gathering tonight as I have said, there are many minds concentrated upon your problems; seeing how you cope; understanding your weaknesses and being prepared to help you when you need help. To curb the extremes; to temper your feelings with a little common sense and advice; to encourage you and to uplift you for your minds are often so wayward and given to following the merest whim. And we try to raise you up above to expect a little better of yourselves. The air about you is filled with spirit, it is the essence of life, it brings you motivation, and it is the power behind everything: That which moves the worlds and that which tends to the smallest flower and so spirit, mighty though it is, is yours to command. That, in your deepest self you know and understand, the purpose for which you were born and that deeper self knows and that which is given to you as days go by is your spiritual agenda. It is for you to deal with; to experiment with; to learn from; to combat and to overcome. And that which has been given to you by your own spiritual self is for you and you alone and when you feel that the world has been unfair or treated you badly, I want you to remember this; that for you the world is of your own making. It is your teacher and your guide that you might learn and understand the things that your soul needs for its very growth. And in coming to you I want you to consider this profound truth, that everything is sent that you might understand the spiritual: Not to hurt you or harm you or knock you down but to teach and uplift and through your dark moments to bring you light for this is the paradox my friends, only by experiencing the darkness can we understand the light. And so I want you to take a new view on things, to meditate perhaps, to think about your position in the world and your attitude to it, and to learn from my words that you are truly blessed because you are understanding. You can see the way lighted before you and your friends walk with you that you may gain the best from your experiences. And when you feel down and under pressure, when you feel that circumstances are not what you would wish, not what you asked for, not what you desire, remember that we are with you and we will teach you that which you need to learn. And we will help you to overcome and be strong, and through that to feel that upliftment and the glorious freedom which is the freedom of the spirit. November 1994.

LAUGHTER.

Good evening. Bright and gay, full of life, of promise and hope, this is how we want you to be, not solemn, serious and downcast. Your circle is a joyous occasion, full of laughter, full of energy, full of giving and sharing and compensating for each other's problems. When one is down and the others are buoyant and joining together in merriment this is how we see you for this is how we are. Living is a serious business I hear you say and we should be serious about it. That is true but being serious never forbade a smile or happy laughter. Create within yourselves a wellspring of happiness, a cheerfulness, an optimism. Be prepared to fight the good fight with humour as your sword. Steer clear of serious things that bring you no benefit, which take your mind away from the joy of living. And if I sound irresponsible I am not for the happiness which you will feel, the joy that you will give will reveal to you a world that is a positive one, a certain one; irrespective of failure; irrespective of pressures and problems. There is another side to life, which brings in its wake a certain outlook, a certain frame of mind that is easier to cope with, which has more strength and which has more promise than that which entraps your mind in problems that can never be resolved. And so be happy; be prepared to smile, to give yourselves a treat for on this side we are full of merriment. We see you downcast at times and we want to make you laugh for laughter is a medicine; it brings into your heart a feeling and a joy that can resist the greatest of pressure. In the world there are many serious issues to face, there are many bad things happening and we would council you to do your best wherever you can and yet, there is another view of the world which can be, and is, the province of the spiritual. And through all these events there is a silver thread running which one day will bring the sufferers out into the sunlight which will be a thousand fold brighter than their darkest moment. I bring you peace. I bring you love but most of all I bring you laughter. God bless. April 1995.

HELP FROM ABOVE.

In the world of spirit we blend together in a way that is unimaginable to you. As one we work and think, tending our sheep, watching the fortunes of one and then another, coming into their lives and bringing them, we hope, a little glimmer, a little understanding: Something which will keep them going, that will arm them against the battles they have to fight and which will give them insights into their own being and that of their fellow man. Our work is never done because we never need rest. Always we are coming to the rescue, always we are fighting fires, and always we are forgetting our own pleasures that we might be of service to you and give of our best. We seek to serve, just as you should in your lives, in honour and in love, promoting that spirituality which is forgotten in this modern age. Man has need of something to cling too and yet only materialism seems to fill that space. I come to you with a comparison between the two states of being, the spiritual and the material: That which occupies your mind time, rules your very being and to which you turn your attention and that which is hidden which is of greater value and which will bring you strength if you look for it. I cannot find the words to express the joy and the beauty and the wonder that is the world of spirit, the world of the spiritual. It is a hidden knowledge that is there for all and yet is rarely seized upon. Mankind looks to the earth instead of to the stars and we tell you that there is such a great power, a wonderful wisdom and glory in that which is of the spiritual. It will lighten your lives, it will lighten your burdens and it will illuminate your soul like the rainbows or the rays of sunshine if only you can catch hold of it. But it is there, real and tangible and we bring it every time we come. We saturate your auras with it and yet still you are filled with your earthly preoccupations, your worries and your woes. But let me tell you that if only you can catch hold of that which is of the spiritual then you will see a transformation. Bring us in with your thoughts, reach out to us and we will share them with you for where we are there can be no darkness. It is in power I come, the power of the Father, and the power of the community of souls who work for the light, for the gracious being we call God. The Heavenly father rains down upon you goodness all of your lives and yet you feel it not. The sense of loving and belonging, the sense of being which you receive from Him one day will be yours and you will understand as we understand. I come in the name of the Lord. God Bless. September 1993.

GOOD AND BAD INFLUENCES.
Whilst we cry out for the help of human beings in our quest to bring knowledge to mankind and to help him on the road, in the world of spirit there are many who would do the reverse, who would harm, who would bring low through ridicule and insensitivity. This is the result of free will which operates on our side just as it does on yours. These misguided souls enter into the lives of those individuals who will listen to them and will act upon their impressions, the thoughts that they give them. And it is for that individual to choose to listen or not to listen for every man has a choice and in

entertaining thoughts which have a low moral tone they open themselves up to influences that are bad for them, that will drive them lower and will make their life harder. In the world of spirit we come to these souls in order that we might help them as we help you, but have great difficulty in getting them to listen to us. In our world we have peace and harmony. In their world there is discord and strife and until they learn to overcome their feelings of hatred and jealousy, of envy and greed, then they will have to suffer the feelings and the anxieties that are generated by those in whose company they exist. And so when we say be careful of your thoughts we have another reason for doing so that these individuals who are so misguided are not allowed a foothold within your mind that they will be repelled by good thoughts and good actions, that they will perhaps learn by example but more importantly that you will be protected and kept safe from influences that would make your life harder and more difficult. In the world of spirit then there are many who would harm you just as there are many who would help and it is for you to choose. Entertain only thoughts of a higher nature and this will be your protection. The wonderful vibrations that accompany a spirit of light give warmth and comfort to all who come into contact with this wondrous being.   September 2003

LOVE.
Good evening. Love is the greatest gift that we can posses: It makes us feel that everything is all right; it conquers fears; enhances the moment; reaches into the innermost depths of our being, and keeps us in a frame of mind which says I can and I will. The positive outlook that love creates allows us to achieve great things: Love cannot be conquered by the sword, nor brought low by circumstance, it is forgiving and enriching. It speaks volumes about the world and yet it takes so little effort that by the time we are absorbed by it's bounty it has tremendous gifts to offer; reaching out into the empty space; propelling us forward in our daily life and helping us

through the most difficult periods. When we feel love in our hearts we are ready to begin to forget: We feel the happiness and the pleasure of the moment; we experience a great uplift which carries us as on wings of prayer through all of our troubles, regardless of life's fortunes, and in spite of the wrongs that have been done to us. Only when love is in the heart are we able to truly say that we are the children of God.

February. 2003.

IN THE BEGINNING.

In the beginning there were many souls who did come together to put forward a new plan of existence, who did take the requirements of the soul for growth, that it might learn through a series of incarnations, experiences set in different scenarios, that it might learn to understand that which was different from itself. In coming to this conclusion they understood the need for the soul to grow and to experience and to make progress and so they set about their task of making that possible. Through effort and enquiry they did fashion new planes of existence upon which spirit could play which was called physical matter. And that did mean that while spirit is immersed in that new concept it would have no understanding of it's origins nor of it's purpose but would be deliberately deprived of all knowledge and all understanding that it might come to it's own conclusions and thereby face itself by contradiction, and experience and understanding. And by this means spirit would look at life from other points of view; different concepts; different ways of looking at things; different ways of understanding. And whilst immersed in matter would have to strive in a way that was not necessary in the spirit that would bring it pressure; pain; misery; depression and all of the things that are absent in the realms of spirit. By this means there would be an understanding of the true meaning of peace for without one the other would not be fully understood

And as spirit entered into matter in that fashion it found a great deal more satisfaction that it has hitherto experienced in a world where nothing was difficult, where everything was available and all things were possible. And so in enriching this spiritual point of view through immersion in matter, it also enriched the lives of those in the world of spirit who were able to share in this evolutionary process. Therefore the general level of understanding was increased as each generation arrived back into the realms of spirit and as each new generation works in the realms of matter for the improvement of the race and the happiness of the individual.

April. 2003.

(If the idea of the mighty universe being designed sounds highly improbable, according to physicist, astronomer and mathematician Sir James Jeans FRS, 'The universe begins to look more like a great thought than like a great machine.'..'...or for want of a better word we describe as mathematical.') (P137/138. 'The Mysterious Universe.' Cambridge University Press. 1930.)

THE GRANDEUR OF THE UNIVERSE.

Put before you the grandeur of the universe, this is the kingdom of heaven in all its glory; the way it is constructed; the thought behind it; the purpose; the coming together of many ideas; propositions and discussions. Open hearted; making pace with each new idea; excitement at its fulfilment; determination that the universe would be a place of beauty as well as a place of work; endeavour; adventure and a sense of achievement when it was finished. Learning to correct and to change circumstances to fit in with the requirements of man; making sure that he did not suffer because of ill-thought-out ideas. Correcting and terminating some lines of thought which did not work which had no purpose. In creating the brilliance of some of the concepts; supercharging them; bringing them forth out of the morass of ideas; the chaos of conflicting arguments and designs. Working as a team; a great thought; a great idea, superlatives really don't cover the description of the mighty universe and of all the things that are in it. November 2014.

SEEKING TO UNDERSTAND.
Yes. Love will find a way, where there are problems there are always solutions. It is in the nature of man to seek to know, to understand, and if that understanding is in the material world then he will search until he thinks he understands. If that understanding is in the spiritual world he will search until he thinks he understands. In searching he looks for answers and in looking for answers he considers many things. If his search continues he begins to grow and he begins to understand but if his search ends, if he is satisfied with his conclusions then he ceases to grow and he ceases to understand that in opening up the door one must never close it. It must be always open to new and exciting and challenging ideas for life is never what it appears to be it always has something up its sleeve; the unexpected; the unforeseen; the unknown. And this is the richness of living; that quality which keeps us going on throughout all eternity; seeking to understand, seeking to overcome, seeking to know what it is we are looking for and so when people stop looking they become sceptical and they are very pleased with themselves because they think they have found all the answers. October 2000.

VICTIMS OF CIRCUMSTANCE.
Good evening, rough justice, this is what people find in this world however, in the spirit word there is a different view of things where everything is taken account of, nothing is out of place or is suffered that does not have a reason, a purpose and a sense of direction. And so when you feel anguish, when you see people who are treated badly who seem to be in circumstances that are oppressing them remember always that there is a plan and a purpose for each and every one of

us. That we might get the best from our earthly lives; understand the depths of our own character; come to terms with what troubles us and appreciate what others are going through. In the mean time there is much to be done much to be achieved and eventually we each of us will confront that which troubles us; that which threatens to drag us down; that which makes us what we are. For all over the world souls are experiencing life in so many different ways that they seem to be victims of circumstance randomly chosen by fate to under go the most punishing experiences; the most terrifying ordeals and the most heartbreaking scenarios: Stories which make you want to weep and bring you great sadness and pain. But the work that these souls are doing is cathartic; is mind changing; is strengthening and giving them an opportunity to grow. While it seems to us as onlookers the result of bad luck, a chance in a million, in the spirit word there will be much rejoicing upon each individual's return. Enriched and invigorated they have overcome their worst fears having appreciated what others have gone through. They have seen for themselves how their actions caused a reaction or perhaps how they reacted themselves to the circumstances in which they found themselves. And whilst it may seem to you to be a cruel and pointless exercise, life in all its many facets has an underlying purpose which is greater than anything you could ever imagine. It is more wonderful than all of the most beautiful moments put together because of the happiness which results from a lifetime of experience in which many things are learned: It is rich in understanding, spiritual knowledge, and strength of character. In time you will understand the meaning of life at its deepest level, at its most poignant where the cross that each of us has to bear is shown to be the most magnificent part of our experience. It will put the brightest moments in the shade because of the depth of its meaning and the quality of the experience which makes us what we are. Come now into the light and share with us one of the brighter periods of your life where all is as it should be and make that change for the better which will bring you the fulfilment that you crave. From us to you, God bless. 19th April 2007

TURNING POINTS.

In every lifetime, there is a turning point, a time of new understanding and different actions: A contemplative period that allows the individual a change of perspective, a new avenue of thought, of direction, and of purpose. When these turning points come they are a revelation, they are the culmination of many years of action and reaction. And now the time comes when that sequence of events has fulfilled its purpose and the individual must move on, must make a new turning along a different avenue with different objectives and more fulfilling dreams. It has come full circle for the energy that has been put into that particular line of thought has expired, it has done its job, it has met the purpose and the result has been obtained that was so desired in the beginning. In coming to a turning point each of us is blessed because it is in a sense a successful outcome: A change of outmoded attitudes, clearing out the attic, dispensing with the old and bringing in the new. All of us have these periods and everyone looking back can recognise what they were. It is when our thinking changes like this that we go forward with a lighter step, a greater determination, a feeling of achievement, and an optimism that there has come an opportunity for something new. Our understanding has grown and our need is to move on, to refresh our minds in pastures new. All the while, we are experiencing the culmination of many years of focussing upon one way of doing things, of being a slave to a particular set of values or attitudes and all at once we decide to discard them. We turn the key and open the lock and we release that which has transfixed our minds, which has captivated our reason, which has demanded our understanding and now the turning point comes and we see a new vista of splendid opportunities; of dreams come true; of ambitions; of enterprise; of hope and anticipation. And we come to you tonight in the knowledge that you are seeking change within yourself, desiring the opportunity to move forward, to set your mind free and to enter upon the next phase that you might create for yourself a new sense of purpose and determination and hope. And in the fullness of time each of us sees that, that which has captivated our minds and enticed us away from what might have been was but a shadow, an experience, a fulfilment of an idea. Wherein the change is completed and there is a feeling of achievement; a sense of fulfilment; of contentment and at the same time we desire that things will change. Come with us on a journey, it will be a magnificent ride. Then at the end of our days when we look back we will see the purpose of our lives and understand that the turning points were milestones. That the journey between them was one of endeavour, coming to grips with that which troubled us; examining both ourselves and the situation and being prepared to work it out. Love will bring you the things you need, give yourself a chance, fulfilling times are ahead. God bless. September 2003.

Because your mind is king, only when you ask can we help and even then we cannot allow you to avoid that which must be learned, that which must be experienced. 11th April 2013.

LIFT YOUR MIND.

Earthly pleasures are but fleeting and have no power or substance they are however a catalyst by which you can attain that spiritual light and love and so you must take hold of that which is so fleeting and make it your own. Forge ahead in the right direction, see how easy it is to leave your troubles behind and come with me to paradise. The God which is within you is the part of you that is the central core of your being it has mastery over you, over your senses and your being and yet it plays no part in your life save to monitor and to watch closely how you react to the various circumstances. And if it thinks you are over burdened it will help and then you will see the mysterious power of God at work, but for you a promise, if you will but lift your mind one small degree then God will multiply that by a 100 or even a 1000 times. October 2,000.

SMALL PACKAGES.
Life comes in small packages, each one being opened as a surprise, taking over the thoughts for a while until that period is expended and a new package comes along. Sometimes the packages are big, sometimes they are small, sometimes they are less frequent but always they are a surprise, never predictable and rarely foreseen. When they do come they can be a joy but some people get packages which are less welcome. And all through life we encounter these phases, these periods, these special moments that teach us, that lead us forward from one experience to the next. Then when we are finished, and we look back along the line we see that each package was a gift from God, sent that we might experience the joy of its making. That we might experience the purpose for which it was given to us; that we might learn to understand that the contents were special and even if not welcome, brought something that improved our lives; that did make us what we are; that did enhance our journey and bring us the richness that is the joy of living. For without these different phases there would be a meaningless and bland existence from which we would gain nothing, through which we would go eternally in our quest for meaning. And so these various gifts from God are there to bring richness into our lives; to enhance our understanding; to give us cause to love each other because of our difficulties; to understand each other despite our differences and to share the companionship that we give to each other through our

individuality and our separate experiences: Always going forward helping one another and making progress through the ups and downs, the twists and turns of the ever present love of God. When our lives are over and we see how we have fared then we will understand that the love of God was with us every step of the way enhancing and enriching our lives. March 2003.

THE WORK OF THE SPIRIT.

Good evening. The world is a better place for the presence of those who believe in God. The work of the spirit is manifold in various strata beginning with the earth itself and radiating outwards to the various spheres that surround the earth both light and dark and in this huge network of concern, of activity, of love and dedication, there are many individual helpers who are tested and tried as they struggle with their charges endeavouring to bring each one into the light. The love of God is with each and every one of you, His care and attention is focussed upon every individual and each soul within His keeping. Nothing is over looked, nor is there any part of the process that is neglected or forgotten. Souls who come to us seeking the light will find that their lives are transformed, that the process of healing begins and the opportunity to grow increases. Everyone who comes to us is taken through an initiation, a period of trial where activities are measured in order that we might understand the capability of our charges: The strengths and the weaknesses, the need to overcome that which holds them back, that which prevents them from being the shining light which we know that they are. In our work we are dedicated to the life plan of the individual; making it work; correcting it; putting right that which is wrong; over coming obstacles that prevent the fulfilment that was meant to be; teaching lessons and seeing the results. It is all very complicated but very logical for in growth we need application, dedication, determination and weak though these may be we fan the flames; we strengthen the will; we help the weary, and we bring light to those in darkness. This is the voice of Friedrick. I come to you that you might understand our mission, that you might be able to take part in the work we do; the saving of souls; the calming of minds and sewing the seeds of determination and hope. Work is plentiful and the needs are many but on our side we never tire, we undertake all tasks, confront all problems and dedicate ourselves to the procurement of happiness. The world is at your elbow bring it the good news. Help them understand that the care and attention that is lavished upon them will bring them into the light, will help them through the darkest moments and will keep them safe and unharmed. God is with you never forget that. - Try to overcome the tendency to think in terms that cause despair, that bring you unhappiness and endeavour always to raise the stakes. Fill your heart with joy to make yourself aware of the more spiritual aspects of living so that you might enjoy each day, each hour each moment and draw from that strength when times become difficult. It is for you to try to conquer, to overcome. It is for us to light the way, to give you hope, to bring you joy and fulfilment. God bless. **January 2004.**

THE CHRIST WITHIN.
The tenor of my talk tonight is in terms of the Christ which is within each of you, which reflects the goodness and the glory of God; the love and the harmony and the pleasure in things spiritual; and the coming together of all minds as one, peacefully, in tranquillity and harmony. For the Christ spirit is in essence the power of God within each of us, that which was sent that we might be apportioned some of the Father's power and greatness, that which gives us life and purpose and humility. In every one of us there is this spark of the divine: His light illuminates ages past, it lights the way towards the future, and it is the power of life itself. It is the gardener working in the garden offering His services, tending the flowers, and bringing in the harvest: It is all of you added

together and yet separate. In each lifetime there is a golden thread, a sense of belonging, an opportunity to follow that light, and yet, some people alienate themselves from it, reject it, and separate their lives from that spark of the divine and become as different people. And then begins the long trek to find that which was given freely, to rejoin that spark of goodness, to open up into the light to recreate within themselves that which was there at the beginning. If everyone of you could do this how joyful you would be for the Master which is within each of us looks to you, looks after you, keeps you safe, and tries His best to make you grow strong in His image. The care He gives to you, His single mindedness, it is full of purpose. He creates for you a garden in which your soul can dwell, He prunes you, He waters you, He sets your face towards the sun, and when you are fully grown, He takes you and He places you in a prime position in His garden. But you have the feeling that you are neglected and forgotten, that there is no one there looking after you, that you are lost and have no purpose and yet I tell you that that beautiful light is there, ever present, ever concerned with your welfare, ever loving and kind and He sees to it that your best interests are uppermost. He follows His plan for you and directs the course of events that you might blossom, that you might bloom in all your glory and give to Him the pleasure that the gardener seeks. I tell you friends never to be downcast for you are never alone. The strength and the power that is within you is beyond all measure. It will keep you safe forever and ever. In His name I come.

September 1994.

WHEN THINGS GO WRONG.

It is natural that sometimes things will go wrong and will not always be perfectly at peace and stable but the necessity is that these events give colour and meaning to a life that would otherwise be bland and pointless. So spend a little time with us in your thoughts and do your very best.

Every time you breathe you go forward; the passage of time in itself is a movement because in every event there is change: Even the negative moments are the positive ones in disguise. The whole purpose of living is to confront the negative, to be so familiar with it so that it pales into insignificance and becomes a positive attribute; a stepping stone on the way to happiness; a means by which we understand the things that we do. And, when we are finished with this earthly plane, the negative things will have far more value than the positive because the positive was often seen as the time when things were going well, when there was no pressure to achieve or to perform but the negative was the drive the ambition the going forward, and so my friend things are not always as they seem. That time when you felt so low was a turning point and each time you return to that state of mind it is a reminder that you have turned away from it and you have grown stronger. The habit to be positive becomes more ingrained and even though you might doubt yourself, might look over the years with despair, you have made great strides within yourself and will soon reject the bitterness and the emptiness which has filled your mind these recent years. In its place will come achievement and optimism, a happiness beyond all measure for you have deserved it. There have been moments when you have wanted to go forward more than anything and yet your negativity held you back and then in the course of time you suddenly realised that you have moved, that we have listened to your prayers, that you had created within yourself a desire and that desire had propelled you forward. For only when there is a desire for change will change come, it is a natural law, it is an obvious result of a change of attitude.

FEELINGS

Tonight we will consider feelings. Feelings can be joyful, they can be awesome but they can be terrible in their vengeance and regret and all the kinds of things that we have experienced in life so managing feelings is a must in this world. You all have your own ups and downs, experiences where you haven't controlled your feelings, where they have taken over; experiences where you have kept silent when you needed to though managing feelings can be a rocky road: Also they are the joy in living; beautiful objects; beautiful scenes and nice people. When we get good feelings we can be on top of the world and so it is good to protect them, to guard against going into the pit of despair; looking on the black side; being glum and disappointed. Easier said than done you might say but it is something which is a life-long quest. – To manage the feelings, to manage the secret of happiness, of peace, quiet and security amidst the storm of life. We in our world know only too well the pitfalls which have come about through lack of management of feelings. Jumping in without thinking, reacting too violently when we disagree and being generally all at sea with ourselves because something has upset us therefore we must look for the calm within the storm: Remembering good things and happy things when we are threatened with instability and disappointment and all in all trying to start the day with some happy thoughts. Think of good things, helpful things and that always works. Where you feel destructive and resentful and where you disagree with people that is often the path to disappointment and anger. And so I come to you trying to help you think of that word love, that all-embracing word that brings delight and happiness to mankind. If only it were everywhere but it is often hidden, kept secret, away from public gaze. And if we could all show the joy and happiness which is there for us it spreads; it is very infectious and it helps other people to lift their spirits; to make them feel happier; more confident and at the end of the day satisfied that things have gone well. And so we bring to you these thoughts. Try to be happy, try to be confident, and try to forgive yourself when you do make a mistake for mistakes are ways of learning and bringing you to a higher level. When you see your friends show them a smile, give them a hug and show them thoughtfulness. Be with them in their troubles, and try to help and lift them when they are down just as when we come to you we do our best when you are down. So look to these thoughts, and lift your minds above the everyday and be with us in our delight and our love for mankind. I give you these words in the name of The Lord. God Bless. 27th October 2015.

A SUGAR AND SPICE WORLD.

You will notice that writers have always put forth a view of the spirit world as a home from home, a sugar and spice world where nothing is learned and where all experiences are happy ones. And this is how it is with so many people but there are different degrees of happiness and knowledge and of understanding and these will present themselves to all who come to our world. And they will have to absorb and ponder and read and learn and think and specialise in this or that till they too are rounded individuals blessed with the greater knowledge that each life brings to the party. January 2013.

LIVING IN HARMONY.
The Kingdom of Heaven is a wondrous place: We live in harmony, we get on well together and we swap stories and make amends. There is much laughter and comradeship and coming together as friends by opening doors and seeing one another's point of view, by explaining and coming terms with and learning to understand those who are sometimes very different from us: Those who have a different way of looking at life and cannot perhaps get a grip on reality; who make it hard for themselves and don't know which way to turn. But

all is levelled in the Spirit World as there are many helpers, many guides and many strands of thought which will lead the doubtful into the light with love in abundance. March 2016.

THE SPIRIT WORLD.

You wish to have a physical description of the spirit world. You are intent upon creating an image which is of the physical but we must council you against this for though there are many glowing treaties upon worlds which are of the spiritual they lack the essence of true reality which is that these places are so much intertwined with the feelings and the personality of those who live there. We are not divorced from these scenes we are an integral part of them and so it is impossible to imagine the great splendour and beauty which is present at these various places when simply presented with a visual picture. -

It is worth considering the viewpoint of those who reach out to you to encompass your mind and for a minute try to understand that their work is of a purely mental character. It is the aspiration of someone who is trying to help mankind in whatever way he can and there are many avenues of thought, many paths of consciousness. It is all a question of experience, of desire, of taking the opportunity which presents itself and as we sojourn these realms of the purely spiritual we realise that there is that essence within us which is eternal, which is of Him who created all, though it is as much a mystery to us as it is to you.

A JOURNEY OF ENLIGHTENMENT.

In these cities of splendour and of beauty there are many who work in harmony and dedication to inspire those in the realms below and in doing so they link their minds and their very being that they might charge their fellow men with the necessary power to overcome and to meet head on those difficulties of which life is full. -

The spiritual worlds are in essence the epitome of all that is good and true. They are a reflection of that which is highest in man and his environment. We are in ourselves but a pale reflection of that which is of God. His message to us is one that is spiritual, which is an insight into causes, and effects that bring us knowledge of ourselves and the circumstances that surround us. In the spiritual world there are places which reflect each of these attributes: They are manifestations encompassing a certain outlook, a certain feeling, a certain train of thought, and these places are knitted together rather loosely and, as we progress, we journey from one level to another so that we can express ourselves in different regions. As we go we leave behind our miss-understandings and our misapprehensions and we follow onto something that is of a more enlightened state, a greater understanding. And so we progress slowly through the different regions until we arrive at a threshold, which is the beginning of a New World. In each of these places there are peculiarities, there are insights into what makes man what he is and what troubles him and these regions are tailor-made to cater for the very essence of the problem and of overcoming it. Each is a place of special endeavour to come to terms with that aspect of thinking, of living, with which it is concerned. As we move about our world we encounter each of these regions. We can take our time there and learn to come to terms with the things we are encountering and all in all there are always things to be learned; to be understood; to be taken account of and so whilst there are places there are also regions and worlds. As we gain understanding we leave behind those particular aspects which have troubled us and move onto something which is more generalised and at the end of the day we are charged with the mission to accelerate man's understanding by bringing him into the knowledge of what the journalists call, 'The peace that passeth all understanding.'

February 1990.

CHANGING OUR AFINITY WITH THE SPIRIT WORLD.

The endeavours of those on this side of life to bring certain people into a new way of thinking are tremendous. Great thought is brought to bear sometimes and much ingenuity to achieve a certain end; to bring the soul back into the fold and into a fairer land for that is what we are talking about. The elevation that is reached, the thought patterns, are akin to certain planes, certain regions in our world and as we work with people so they change their affinity and become more in tune with the higher planes and with different regions of thought. August 1991.

A WORLD OF INSIGHTS.

We bring an understanding to mankind which is of value and which has been gained at some expense, that which we have learned by trial and error and by observation. We then have a greater, overall understanding that we can put forward as a solution to many of the more involved problems in the way of sending our thoughts to those who are receptive. We see how difficult it is for some people to comprehend certain basic things and we help them to come to those conclusions that will take them forward. If our world were purely composed of substances that were of harmony we would be in a different sphere completely. There are bound to be differences and incongruities that have to be met with and understood. Though the difference may not be jarring, it may not be a great one, there are always things to be taken account of, people to discuss things with and to counter one's own arguments. Now if you were trying to see how easy it is for a person to come into the new light, the new thinking, - we are trying to tell you that the spirit world is a world of beauty but also a world of insights. It is not the essence of a fairy land where all is perfect it is a place of work where we are learning to understand; where we strive; where we counter each other's arguments and come to terms with each other's interests until we have grown in the same way as you do on earth. It is not all sugar and spice though, let it be said, there are many who are not progressed at all and will not enter this sphere until they do so however, there are plenty of disagreements to be met with in various activities and spheres which we can travel to and where we can meet with those who are thinking along different lines. Therefore we are not always in the position of harmony and agreement. As with earth you have lots of ideas and actions it is so in the spirit world. There are many different sides to an argument and there are many different people with different personalities therefore we are not the harmonious whole that you might think is the blandness of uniformity. And in this difference of opinion there is a new element to be taken account of which is speaking to a person maybe in terms that may be threatening but which in this context would simply be an effort to understand. It will not be the disharmony of earth where violence might be the result. And so the spirit world, being composed of many facets, many arguments is in essence a kaleidoscope of various views and aspects and its beauty is unsurpassed. Though there may be regions of comparatively simple outlook, the natural beauty of that attitude is displayed in the surrounding atmosphere.

February 1990.

THE WORLD OF SPIRIT.

When you reach the world of spirit your love will be increased a thousand fold. You will love and be loved. You will share in the love and the harmony which is the spirit world and there you will see how you are repaid for all those deeds you have done.

Looking for riches within your own activities and multiplying them a thousand fold will be but a pale reflection of that which awaits those who arrive in the world of spirit where everyone is working that mankind will feel something and that their work is echoed throughout the spheres even to the very depths. In harmony they work for there is great power where many are gathered together and there is the wondrous beauty of these realms where the whole atmosphere is of a spiritual nature. December. 1990

The simple fact is that there are many insights into the world of spirit that can be brought forward as the truth and when you have finished analysing you have naught but the personal viewpoint and speculation; and the substance is as a fairy tale insubstantial wispy and unreal. But the spirit world is none of these things. It is tangible, it is real, it is powerful, it is beautiful, it is everything that anyone could hope for both in appearance and in creating a feeling of well being that transcends any of the joys ever felt on earth. There can only be one point of view when it comes to the spiritual and as the spiritual is the substance of all things it is to the spiritual you must look for your descriptions of the world of spirits. There are many avenues along which the mind can travel and there are many places in the spirit world but there is only one avenue that leads to God. 'Where many are gathered together there shall I be,' and in the realms of the spiritual there are many avenues that take one on a roundabout journey through landscapes fair and wonderful and even into the realms of darkness but at the end of them all there is only one golden light and that is the light of God. Through these experiences these different routes these different pathways to the living God, we grow and we experience and we understand that which we did not understand before. We gain wisdom and the experience gives us the grounding in what it is like to be a human being, an individual, a separate person with separate ideas with separate choices with separate wishes and with separate faults. Without these various pathways we would never reach that exalted position that infusion with God that comes after an eternity of trekking through countless numbers of experiences and places and of riches untold; that brings the wisdom that we need to complete our journey. Yes, suspend belief for a moment, take upon yourself for a while my words that I bring to you in humility that you might consider them, that you might take them for your own that you might be able to write them down to appeal to others who need to understand. There are many facets to the question of philosophy, all kinds of subjects on which we could discourse, but the greatest of these is love for love is at the centre of everything. It is the driving force which pushes you forward and which takes you through those experiences which you need for your progression. In life we find the central core of existence the road to which all roads must return and no matter how far we stray away from that central pathway, there is a voice calling us back, entreating us to be at one with that glorious power of love and love is the way of the Father. November 2,000

INDIVIDUALITY.
The profits that man makes by being on earth are incalculable they bring him joy love and understanding and free him from his singular world in Paradise. This allows him to develop his own muscles; his own mind; his own being and his own line of thought and this without intrusion from other beings which is a thing in itself worth contemplating. How are we to be individuals if we are forever in the company of like minds? - Teaching us yes, but being with us all of the time is not conducive to the stress and the strains of decision making; choosing; learning through trial and error and becoming an individual centred around a lot of personal experience. August 2015.

THE SPIRITUAL REALMS.

The spiritual realms are indeed realms of great beauty; they are indescribable. In essence they are a compound of all that is good in man, reflected into space they form an aura which is to those on that plane solid. And, as indeed we progress, that purity of light that infuses the spiritual body and mind becomes more and more pure. In the further reaches of these regions, which are to many beyond bounds, there are wonders yet unknown. In these realms of light dwell those who have progressed so far that man has been left far behind but still these great beings encompass all that is good in man. In these reflections we find traits of imperfection and as the light becomes purer, it infuses the spiritual body and the spiritual mind bringing about a greater harmony and a greater longing for that nearness to the Father. And the great beings who once trod the path of earth, and who now inhabit these spheres of light, take all in their prayer who come to them for help and guidance. No one is forgotten and all mankind is encompassed within the very highest as heaven is a place for those that dwell there. These heavenly realms are the very fount of man's knowledge and man's spiritual understanding; for all which is of the spiritual is reflected back into the earth and is seen by those who are receptive; those who take upon themselves the mantle of the spiritual and are able to come into tune with the realms of light to cause them to resonate within their surroundings, that which is of the spiritual. And the realms of light are in the very essence of the Father. And He who dwells there is ever aware of His presence and being nearer to Him takes upon himself that which is of the work of the highest. The very presence of His love spurs each soul to attain that which is greater and that which is higher ever onwards and upwards and as these realms of light are the footstool of the Father so too do the realms of light begin to penetrate further towards earth. And mankind will be lifted out of the darkness of ignorance and into the light and in time will feel that loving care even as those in heaven do feel. (*Can we describe it more physically?*) In physical terms these realms are more difficult to describe, their very atmosphere is of the spiritual. The clothes which are worn and the bodies which are inhabited are of that plane and infused with the feeling of love, with the desire to serve and with the humility of all who are very spiritual. And that which is of landscape that surrounds them is of such magnificence that the word beauty hardly seems adequate to describe the wonders that await those who reach the higher spheres. In everything and in every way these wondrous places emit that which is the very essence of the Father and gives to the inhabitants there a strength and an insight which is difficult to comprehend from our point of view. As we come nearer to the light so it draws us forward and those who return to tell of such wondrous sights do so filled with a renewed strength and vigour, with renewed love and filled with the wonder of that place. We would lay down our very lives that those in the world could glimpse the wondrous beauties of these realms. December 1988.

CONSCIENCE

There are many roads down which the mind can travel, some enlightened, some a diversion, others pretty horrid and not nice places to visit. Those who are intent on harming others who disagree with them so strongly that they would fight to a bitter end, are destined for the dark regions of the mind. They reach into their conscience and what they find there is terrifying: Regrets; actions that cannot be undone; harm: hurt; and unpleasantness but always there is love in abundance. And so if that person looks into the bright area of the mind love will come to the rescue, it will be a natural process. For the lives that we have lived have been many and varied, you cannot say that one soul was all bad or even all good for the different experiences, the pressures and the problems which have been faced have moulded and shaped and distorted sometimes, the viewpoint; the feelings; the attitude and made that person into something perhaps even grotesque: Something which was not foreseen by them in the beginning. And they were tempted away from the light by the attraction of the dark. But the dark found them wandering in the wilderness, not satisfied and not having achieved anything: The life they have lived in disarray with wrong decisions being taken, wrong attitudes being formed and not a great deal of understanding of how these things happened. So when you say that these people feel the full force of their conscience as they come to our side you are in a sense correct. But God always measures and understands and balances the books that those who have been in error will never-the-less, like the prodigal son, have come to the party. Those who insist on their wicked ways, who delight in the pain of others, who are thoughtless and selfish will then feel the chill wind of their own (*conscience or spirit?*) Their own wanting to be perfect in their own eyes. But realising that the way forward was in a different direction and had they taken that direction things would have been brighter and happier and more fulfilling for them. And so you see when we come together in the spirit world we have much to discuss, a lot to put right; things to go over and evaluate. And when you say that these people feel something which is not loving and kind it is a temporary state of mind that they might compare, that they may understand and that they might realise the forgiveness which has been given to them freely, that they may make progress and leave behind the world of man. For in the world of spirit, a world of goodness and light, love is with you all of the time. God bless. March 2016.

THE SPIRITUAL PLANES.
In the spiritual world there are so many dimensions, so many aspects to living, which have not been explored that we cannot possibly say what is beyond the reach of our own experience. There are planes that have never been visited

from this level, in essence they are behind closed doors and yet something of their character rains down upon us. It is as if all heaven was opened up to this glorious power of love.

October. 1991.

In the true spiritual planes there are things that are beyond description, which need to be experienced to be understood. There is an all pervading atmosphere which will take over the very being, which is the individual, to such an extent that it becomes a part of them and is in essence the accumulative personality, accumulative product of the expressions of many lives and as such is more powerful because of its great wisdom and experience. November. 1990.

When finally the planes are reached which require no physical expression there is a deep rapport with the other inhabitants who live in a state of animated thought. It is still true to say that things represent those thoughts for they are the means by which these finer feelings have been experienced have been built up but in their own way these thoughts are purely an expression of something spiritual. When there is complete absorption into the Godhead the things that have created these states of mind are but shadows and the new experience is far beyond our capacity to explain.

October 1991.

THE HIGHER REALMS.

In the higher realms there is a majesty and glory beyond our ken, something which stirs the soul into action, which forms a catalyst with those who are responding from the lower planes and enables that great power of strength to be poured downwards into those darker regions whether they be of earth or of any of the other planes where a cord is struck within the soul of one who would go higher. The individuals who comprise this great stratum of light have progressed for many aeons of time to become those great shining ones and if we are to stand in their shadow we must return to that simplicity of spirit that will bring us the light from within.

THE DARKNESS.

There are planes that are created by thought: terrible regions of misery; areas of complacency and inactivity; all kinds of conditions which have been built out of the minds of men. As we move through these regions we do so that we might learn and to give us insights into what made us what we are. It means that some can come over to our side in a better state more able to tackle the big problems, the big questions and to move on more quickly. Others are trapped in their particular way of thought until they can be freed by circumstances.
August 2,000.

The terrible things that are done in life in the name of God are as the result of ignorance and misunderstanding. It is not for us to judge but to seek to enlighten that the listener may draw something from our words, that their posture may be straighter and taller, that they may anticipate good things and that they might fulfil their dreams in the spiritual by being honest, good, kind and helpful. August 2003.

GUIDANCE.

We are with you constantly: Every avenue down which you walk is overshadowed by the light of God. Not a movement takes place, not a thought; not a feeling within your heart goes unnoticed. We are with you constantly, night and day assessing you, cajoling you, bringing you into line when you stray, sorting out your problems, putting before you the agenda, constantly reminding you of your position and trying to return you to the path: All these things we do in the name of love. We create for you an environment in which you will grow; buffeted by the storm; blown by the wind, but never knocked off course. We teach you, we test you, we try you, but always we love you: We never judge. - It is everyone's wish that you succeed. - If you feel that you have been let down, that the way is not clear, that we have perhaps deserted you when we were needed, fear not friends, for it is all taken account of; your special needs; your weaknesses and your hopes. They are like an open book and we want you to understand that despite your setbacks, you will progress, you will fulfil that need to work with the spiritual; we will never let you go; we will not let you fall, nor will we desert you. - For the power of love is strongest when it is tested. The bonds that you feel around you, restraining you, preventing you from the freedom to go forward, will be released only when you have learned to accept them and to understand them. And all the while you are testing yourself; you are coming to terms; trying to understand; making up your mind; deciding. - All these things are food for the soul that it might grow, that it might be strengthened. And so, though you may feel that the way is not clear, always there is a hand guiding you and taking you forward. If every day could be a perfect day then what would life be? We tell you that you need ups and downs by which you can measure yourself, by which you can appreciate the good times. The contrasts are as much a necessity as is the very food you eat. Take care that you always choose for the best, if in doubt ask, for we are there to serve. We love you always and we come when you are in need. Since we began we have seen many changes in you; the ups and downs; the twists and turns. We have done our best to lead you forward and there are more twists and turns to come but it is not a game of blind man's buff - the way is clear, is marked out and we have a specific goal in mind, so fear not the end will be justified by the means. (?) Forget your troubles and place yourself in the hand of God. Prepare the way and take upon you the light of His mantle. In the name of Jesus Christ I come. I Thank you. God bless. ((J.C. took me by surprise))   **August. 1994.**

UNIVERSAL LOVE.

There is around you a wonderful world put together by the thoughts of man, lovingly crafted, thoughtfully worked out and tried and tested. But not all things can be written in a book because we speak of things that are beyond your understanding, happenings which are hard to describe, events which are so different from anything you have encountered but love in abundance, love is the common denominator, it reaches all levels all worlds, all countries. It never stops giving; it understands all; it reaches all, and so when you are by yourself when you feel detached; low; disinterested just think of love and the giver; the sender and the open heart that has included you within its portals. The feeling of gratitude; of connection, of being able to share the most intimate details and all these things are as the result of love which is the coming together of lots of people in harmony.

11th February 2016

ACCENTUATE THE POSITIVE

Try to examine your thoughts in such a way that you can expel the negative and amplify the positive. Try to enlarge your experience of the good things, try to piece together an attitude of mind which is positive, which is certain, which is sure, which will increase your feeling of happiness: That certainty that you can meet the challenges head on. You have the opportunity to work upon it, to forge ahead, to make that extra effort which is certainly well worthwhile. Seeking that peace, that solace in your own mind will bring you great benefits and will have its effect upon those around you, upon your development and upon your ability to cope. If you can set straight the conditions within your own self, within your own mind, with a little effort you will see, that the sun does shine through, even though there may be the darkest clouds in view, and that these things are just temporary. They pass like shadows and are soon forgotten but they captivate the mind and they threaten to drag you away from that peace which belongs to you.

THEIR OWN LITTLE WORLDS.

Since I began my work to support and to guide I have seen how people's minds work from a different point of view. As an onlooker I can see very clearly how people think and the traps they fall into. The images they present to our side are futile, fruitless and quite bizarre at times. They are very divorced from reality and with a little effort could be dispelled and replaced by an image of peace and beauty, of light and love. And so as I look on and as I see those around you creating their own little worlds, thoughts that are off times not worthy of them, I wonder and I contemplate and try to imagine why they are content to live in such a strange world that is of their own making.

And all the time we are buffeted by the thoughts of others, and by the stresses and strains of living out our lives, and we allow them to rock our little boat, to submerge us and to cast a shadow between us and the sun. If only we could enlarge our vision, if only you could see, as I can see, that greater view of things, that wonderful light, that creative love, that energy, that strength which is always there to be tapped and with a little effort could be reached for. Day-to-day problems play upon the mind, they capture your imagination and if you are not careful take you away from that peace of mind, which should be yours, and so you must always be on your guard. You must always return to that frame of mind which is of peace and tranquillity, of true happiness and joy. Be careful of your thoughts, be wary of them. Try to paint a picture in your own mind which is worthy of you and which will lead you forward into the sunlight. **June 1991.**

BRINGING PEACE INTO YOUR WORLD.

I have just come from the presence of my friends. In their world there is absolute peace, an absence of anger and despair. In your world there is turmoil, dissension and strife. And this is the stark contrast with which we work. The message is, to bring that peace into your world, to infuse it with love and to make it parallel to our world. In the fullness of time this will come about, but not without great effort. The needs of man are threefold; they centre on the spiritual but remain in the material whilst the physical dictates its wants also. The hands which are busy at work in the unseen bring to you a message of hope, caring, sureness and determination. November 1995.

Send out your thoughts to us and we will deal with them and return them to you with love. The work we do is of the greatest importance; the saving of souls; the calming of minds. It is an onerous responsibility and yet we love it dearly. We are invincible. *(I thought, if only we ourselves don't spoil the plan. Then came)* We are certainly unstoppable.-
Your friends are with you. Their wisdom is boundless, their work is divine. They teach you and try you and then you'll be fine. May 1996.

GOD NEVER LEAVES YOU.

God is with you every step of the way; He never leaves you and is constantly by your side. In time of trouble He looks out for you, He supports you and He guides you. In the evening of your years, in the fullness of time, you will understand what it is to guide, and be guided; the pressures; the problems; the set backs; the victories; the patience, and the disappointments. We on our side give much thought to the solving of problems. We enter into the lives of our charges sometimes expecting miracles and we are disappointed when our charges do not respond to our impressions: If they are weak when they should be strong, if they go backwards instead of forwards. And we are overjoyed when there is an unexpected turn of events when those who we are looking after make a sudden leap forward.

January 2003.

THE HIGHER SELF.

When we pray the higher self receives our thoughts and is aware of the sincerity of them and if it cannot answer our prayer it might go to a higher authority. Of its own volition it cannot extract the mind from those conditions before they have been changed; it is contrary to the law, which forbids intervention by God in the affairs of man. There are certain ways through which we must approach these things. It is through the mind we work, through mankind, not through God. God is the instigator, the initiator, the perpetrator; He does not do these things for us. He guides and He councils but never removes from us the necessity to walk forward along the pathway: There is a subtle difference between prayer my son and a God who intervenes at every turn; there are very strict rules on this matter. It is necessary that we understand that there is no unfairness: All is order and is carefully worked out. Where you see suffering, a soul in torment, you must remember that we are watching and waiting for that point in time which will show us that this has been a turning point. We are feeling people and strongly abhor some of the things that are done on earth but to intervene would make a nonsense of living. We are forbidden to extradite these people from their destiny but can take the leading edge of the strain. We can call for help from other human beings and will help in that way if there is a response but we can never, never change the situation from a supernatural viewpoint. It is strictly forbidden. April 1991.

JUDGEMENT.

The spirit world is a world where dreams come true. In all we say and do we create an understanding which fits us for a place in the Kingdom of Heaven. This place is composed of many things. In essence it is the result of our efforts in the past. What we say and do now contributes towards the conditions that we will find when we reach our natural home. If there be light it is the result of a life of unselfishness, if there be dark it is the result of a life which is wasted, which has not helped others but rather hindered them in the course of their duties. -   C 1990.

The world beyond yours is a frightening place, where deeds are seen for what they are. Where attitudes are exposed and underlying reasons brought out into the open so when you think your thoughts and see your visions remember they are created by you that you might come to a conclusion that you might give yourself a message that you might push yourself forward *(Or punish yourself?)* That too! It happens in small doses but we like to help.   7th May 2015
(This seemed to contradict the idea of a world filled with love and harmony so I returned to the subject. I had taken it out of context.)

THE LIVING DREAM. The astral.

These thoughts and occurrences happen when the subject is out of the body but in a state of limbo where the astral lies. The conditions are unstable there and you will find all sorts of dream-like environments; people with issues unresolved; people with fears; people with emotions that have not been kept in check and which when let loose create all kinds of fears and negative impulses. These surroundings are created by the inner mind in sympathy with these negative thoughts. And so when you say that this is contradictory to the idea of heaven filled with love it is just one of the compartments or departments which is in this vast array of human emotions, human conditions.

There are no set routes to the spirit world save the inner reaches of one's own mind which when manifest create these conditions and thought becomes reality. The way that the spirit world is constructed is not in terms of a country but a state of mind the location of which is within the minds of those who inhabit that plane or that condition. They meet there because they think alike; It is not compulsory to pass through these places, it is in effect a condition which is created by those who go there. These conditions are as it were off the beaten track; those who encounter them have strong issues of their own and will soon rectify their environment. They will pass through it but briefly and will recognise that their outlook needs to be changed, and they will go to the place accordingly for which they have fitted themselves. The average person has nothing to fear for the delights of the spirit world are many they provide comfort and upliftment even to the lowliest and they bring to the individual a new outlook a different perspective, a loving and caring environment.

The termination of a life means the end of a particular way of looking at things; everything is brought into sharp focus. The conditions are laid out before the individual who then has the privilege of seeing where he or she went wrong and why. But in this situation there is an over shadowing light or wisdom which leads the person through the scenarios laid before him or her for assessment to create a realisation, to make the transition to the spirit world more acceptable, more reasonable. Having had a change in perspective there are many pastures which are available in which to settle down and enjoy the fruits of their labours.   3rd November 2016.

MAKING PROGRESS.
We cannot go backwards, we cannot remain static, we must forever make progress for it is in the nature of things that we

expand our knowledge; that we blossom like a flower; that we go forth; that we create; that we understand and that we reach out for something better. In this we find a purpose for living, the reason to exist, a happiness that is beyond all measure in the act of creation and yes in giving to others that love which sets them apart from others; that love which gives them strength and helps them on their way. And it is in the company of our fellow men that we go forward giving each other strength when we are down, helping each other when we stumble and growing in the knowledge that Christ is always with us through the darkest days, even until the end. Feast your eyes upon the world and its treasures for in every corner there is a miracle. In every day that passes there is a special moment. In the most depressing of circumstances there is a strange beauty, and in the best of circumstances, when life is sweet there is always that fear, that underlying anxiety that it will not last. And when life is full of woe and misery there is that expectation that happiness will come and so you see the contrasts and the contradictions, the expectations and the doubts are all woven into a rich pattern that we call life. - Everyone and everything together in one harmonious whole, seeking knowledge, seeking understanding, seeking comfort, favour and love from on high. The very stones ring out to proclaim His love; the love of the Creator; the love of Almighty God who sees His children like jewels in a crown, like stars in the firmament glowing brightly independent and yet part of one harmonious whole. -A picture to behold. And it is the greatest of truths that God encapsulates each and everyone of us within His love giving us a special part in His heart making for us a special place in His creation. It is with great love that he gives us our free will but he endows upon us the gift of choice as He takes us through the many and varied paths of discovery into the higher realms. It is for everyone to see that there are golden lights up ahead, each one a spiritual home, each one given with love that we might reach out and take our rightful place in the family of God. It is time to go. I will depart. For now adieu. November 2,000.

FAITH.
The subject for tonight is the question of faith, faith in ones own judgement, in one's fellow human beings and in God's wisdom. If you have not faith then you have doubt, if you have doubt you have uncertainty, if you have uncertainty you are restricted because you cannot make a move for fear of error and in the long term will never achieve that which you set out to do because doubt has clouded your mind. The fear of error has made you stagnant. Without a little faith in yourself, in your God, in your fellow human beings, you will never take that leap to the unknown and you will never forge ahead and fulfil that which you hope to see come to fruition. Look for the silver lining in everything you do. God bless.
November 2,000.

GLOOM AND DESPONDENCY.
Yes. Love gives you the opportunity to move forward. Climb every mountain, reach out to the stars, put your faith in God. Try to help Him to help you and to make you want to love Him more and more for he is reflected in the faces of mankind that you distrust so much and have so little confidence in but He brings you love and assurance that you will be carried on the wings of angels that you might return to His side with the love He has given you multiplied many times. *(Slow and deliberate speaking)* Yes it is a very beautiful thought. When we come to you we want you to be ever mindful that he is taking hold of your hand and leading you in the right direction and when you feel lost or when you feel disturbed or doubtful or down, it is He who is standing by your side giving you the strength and the opportunity to move away from those destructive thoughts that you have made your own. Love returns to its sender. When you give

out love, love is returned when you give out hate, hate is returned. ((*In my case not hate but frustration – wanting to put the world to rights.*)) And so the feelings that you find so hard to bear are a reflection of your own thoughts that you have cast into the wind and have returned that you might find the chill of their force and understand that always where there is action there is a reaction. And if you are to live your life by the light of God then you must learn to reflect that light in your thoughts and in your words then that light will be returned to you in far greater force than that feeble effort that you made when you sent it out. In your lifetime there have been many opportunities to give and receive that gracious power of love. There have been many good thoughts, many happy moments, many pleasing things, and then there were times when you were not so full of love. The world cast its shadow across your mind and in these moments you did send out thoughts of gloom and despondency and these too were returned to you that you might learn to deal with them that you might learn to understand them that you might learn to overcome them. Very soon those thoughts which you had created came back to haunt you, to crowd in on your consciousness to make you even more aware of them. When you feel the chill of your own thoughts it is then that you must make the effort to overcome that which darkens your mind, that which encompasses your soul and creates within you that deep despair. Only when you confront that negative power will it be turned into positive love and all the Angels of Heaven will rejoice that you have created within your being a wellspring of love that was born out of the darkness, because of the darkness, and in spite of the darkness, that you might live once again, in the goodness and in the presence of God. **December 2000.**

BLACK DOG.

The inner conflict drove you into darkness and while you were in that darkness you did explore and try to understand what it meant to you. In your darkness you came to the conclusion that the light was of little value because it was always accompanied by darkness. Now I tell you friend that the darkness is of little value unless it is accompanied by the light. It is for you to come to terms with the facts as they are. We cannot ever cease to exist, it is an impossibility. It is for you to accept that fact, to work to unite those opposing factions within you that pull against each other and create such a force of destruction where there could be power of unity and harmony. It is for you to understand why there can be no darkness without light or light without darkness: It is for you to accept that and to come to terms with it. Try to think of all experiences as being one and the same, the darkness and the light and its different perceptions of the same thing. Events happen; we go through them; we experience them; we move on. What is dark to one is light to another, what is all consuming to one is fuel to drive another forwards. November 2,000.

KIND WORDS.
Good evening. Kind words are never wasted, everything we say and do is measured; a smile, a small gesture, all these have an effect on the company we keep, raising the vibrations, increasing the feeling of wellbeing and friendship, opening the door to new possibilities, to new friendships and new bonds between individuals. Our demeanour is extremely important in the world of man that we may set the scene, that we may improve the tenor of the communications between people, that we may set the pace and increase the desire to be friends, to be kind to each other and to return that warm smile with loving thoughts. For all of us in our workaday world forget these small things and are apt to be wrapped up in our own little world of thought forgetting that there are other people who observe us who are measuring us who are trying to evaluate their relationship with us. And so always we must try to be on our guard try to raise the vibrations: Try

to be happy despite the way we might be inclined to feel, despite the things that would pull us back, and make it a habit of thought to be determined to bring love and friendship into the world. To be good, to act the part, and then perhaps we will believe it ourselves for when we smile it has its effects upon our well being. When we are cheerful it heals the broken heart and when we come together as friends the mirth and laughter is a tonic which will keep out the harshest of conditions, and fortify us for things to come. In our world we feel the warmth of God we feel the love for each other it is in the atmosphere it is in our very being. In your world you are assailed by bad news, by difficult circumstances by problems and troubles which beset your mind. And if you can remember these simple rules; to fix your mind on the good things, to bring joy into your own heart that will bring joy into the hearts of others, then you will feel that the quality of your life improves, life is worth living and love gains mastery over the troubles of the world. We bring these words to you in love and wish you success and love in abundance in the New Year. God bless. 7th January 2008.

THE SILVER LINING
Look for the silver lining. Always there are benefits from anything that happens to you, good or bad. Things are learned and put into perspective to help you make that leap forward. In time you can look back and see the progress that has been made in many small steps, one after the other, and if you were to think about some future state you would never be able to appreciate how those small steps have changed your mind, and in what way. It is only a matter of experience that brings this knowledge and it is very much like that all the way through life. You are progressing, your knowledge is increasing and your understanding grows, but only in small steps: Very rarely is it changed overnight. April 2001.

THE UPS AND DOWNS OF LIFE.
In time you will understand that that which has been given to you was necessary for your progression and did help you to become the person that you envisaged. When you reach the end of the road you will see the true perspective of your life; how you were shaped and moulded by your experiences; what made you tick; what really were the ingredients that were necessary to create that which is your present personality and the ingredients that made you what you are. Like a drum you beat yourself constantly and you make a sound that is inharmonious. Call for us when your spirit is low, cry out for us when your mind is in turmoil, and be with us in your thoughts. When you reach your goal you will be glad of everything that has given you pain, everything that has taxed your ingenuity or troubled your soul for these are the real teachers. Enjoying life is a necessary part of existence, resting stops along the way, but the important thing is that you learn and you experience the contrasts the changes in fortune the ups and downs the troubles and the cares because it is these that give you something to work upon, to push against: It is these that give you the real meaning of life, to progress and live in harmony with yourself and your fellow human beings. The better times may seem the more desirable but they are in fact contrasts and allow you to regain the strength for the things that will follow. Right now you must be strong and determined to overcome your lower self, that which makes you sad, and that which makes you angry. You must learn to control yourself so that you are not at the mercy of these forces that would dash your boat against the rocks. Love gives you every opportunity to find peace within yourself but there are always going to be the tests, the experiences, which in themselves are not difficult but which have within them a certain resistance, an opportunity to progress. Anytime that you feel vulnerable love will step in to show you the way.

Over the way many voices are calling, trying to help you to put behind you all the troubles of the past and to encourage yourself to do the work that I am now doing. February 2003

OPTIMISM.

Yes love brings you many new challenges and if you will persevere those challenges will bring you rich rewards, for it is only with effort and time that you can achieve that which you set out to do. There are many ways of looking at the world: One is with an attitude of fear, and an anticipation of bad things happening all of the time, the other is with optimism and anticipation of good things. It is a matter of perception and to change your perception from one to another is quite a simple trick. What is most difficult is finding the will to do it for when there is a will to be positive it brings with it responsibilities and those responsibilities mean that you have to do things that you are not really prepared to do and you have to take on board actions and plans that you would rather leave alone. And when everything is seen in a negative light you have the excuse you need not to pursue those actions but to lament the lack of results which had those actions been taken would have been positive. In every life there is a main theme, something central to that person's individuality which must be tackled, something very personal, an objective that has to be met despite all other considerations whether successful or not. Flaws in the character are there to be tackled, to be corrected, and they take president over almost everything else in that life. So where success is not achieved in worldly terms success might have been achieved in spiritual terms.

April 2001.

SOMEWHERE OVER THE RAINBOW.

Now come with me on a journey, that journey will take you beyond the stars into another realm where you will see that life is a different concept, that what you have here is simply a fairy tale, an insubstantial and shallow existence that is bringing you the engine by which you can drive yourself forward in this other world, and through which you can gain the things that you so desired, for by struggling with matter, by coming to terms with the circumstances of this world you will make it possible to move higher in the next and to find that fulfilment, that satisfaction that comes with experience and with understanding. In the future you will realise that everything you have given birth to in this world will grow in the next and will reap rewards that are well worth it and that will bring you that satisfaction that you have never had within your earthly body. In the first instance there will be a recognition of all that you have been; of all that you have done; in everything you have attempted; of the failures and of the successes. I want you to understand that as we go forward we need to consolidate all of that earthly knowledge that language of love, the means by which you reach that higher level and then you can use it as a stepping stone by which you can get to an even higher level. The object of the exercise was to give you an understanding of what it is like to pass over and to return to the place from whence you came and what the reaching out will bring you. Now reach out to us in your thoughts. May 2001.

THE LADDER OF SPIRITUALITY.

There can be no going forward without resistance there can be no reaching out without looking back for when you look back you feel the resistance of your own wishing to go forward. It is a natural thing that you must fight and struggle to move, to climb the ladder of spirituality. There can be no easy fixes; no magic cures can overcome those tendencies and habits that you have created or that your life has created for you and it is only when you struggle to overcome those weaknesses that you can begin to move forward.

GOD WALKS WITH US.

It is true that we take the path alone, responsible for our own decisions, taking our own chances, following our own instincts but it is also true that God walks with us on that pathway unseen, unheard and unfelt as we try to come to terms with each new situation; every twist in the road; every pang of pain and each moment of joy. And as the hours roll by He watches and waits; He encourages; He makes plans; He teaches and He guides. Almighty God is so great and all encompassing and yet He follows the progress of each and every one of us, of the myriad of souls in His keeping, and the special relationship He has with each one of them. And as you go on always remember that His hand is at the tiller, His eyes are at the helm and that His love is in your heart.

THE POWER OF LOVE.

Love will bring you freedom from worry and love will allow you the freedom to create. Love will bring you the insights into freedom, this will be the final and most glorious phase, the implementation of all the things that you have desired, the instigation of a new pattern of thought, a more appreciative, a more kindly, more understanding attitude towards your own self and to the conditions in which you find yourself. They are the realities of life that present themselves to each and every one of us; the purpose for which you were born; the process by which you come to a realisation that God is both within and without. - An energy that transcends time and space; that abounds with life and goodness; that brings you the very breath of life; the power to reason and to express yourself, and the patient calm that watches over you as you endeavour to cope with the events of your life. The rebellious thoughts; the failures; the compromises; the insights that you are given help you to cope with all this and much more. Forging a path through life; accumulating experiences; overcoming difficulties;

searching and finding true happiness that is embodied within the events of life. Not hidden from view but on display for all to see, not the privilege of a few people who might be rich but given freely to the poorest and the most helpless. Whilst they enjoy the freedom of love and happiness others will go on searching, trying to find it in all manner of places when in reality it is theirs for the taking. Strengthen your will to succeed, make a bargain with yourself, make the effort and take the chances. December 2001.

A NEW OUTLOOK.

And when you are ready try to bring forth a new outlook into the minds of those who enquire, who delve and question that they might too understand that the path to eternal life is more than just an understanding of the mechanics of surviving death. And that in that survival there are key elements which need to be considered before that day when all that has been; will be called to account. It will be measured and judged with regret with disappointment and sometimes with sorrow that more effort was not made that more knowledge was not gained and that this period on earth had not reaped more rewards in the spiritual. Try to understand that we are not threatening, we are encouraging, we are speaking to the heart and soul of those who will listen that they might catch that spark which once was ignited by the Christ, that would help each individual to have a brighter and happier future and a more satisfying conclusion to his or her life on earth.

January 2002.

CHRIST'S LAWS.

Live in accordance with Christ's laws: From Him draw your strength: In His shadow will you walk. Live within the bounds of possibility, do not expect miracles that have not been worked for, achievements that are not deserved, and rewards which are not earned however this does not mean that the things that you will acquire will not be as valuable as those things of which you have dreamed. The purpose for our life on earth here is not to gain riches or gold it is to gain the power of the spirit: Insights; conclusions; personal achievement, and many things that contribute towards a happy life. In the future we will help you to find the secret of that happiness in giving to others, in achieving your goals and in raising your standards. It is the wish of the Father that you understand the purpose for which you were born. It is the fundamental process by which each of us gains insight into our real self. It is the facing up to the reality; coming to terms with things as they are; achieving things in spite of setbacks and being better because of them. It is not for you to judge the process by which we achieve these things but for you to exploit them on your own behalf; to achieve that spiritual status that brings with it that joy; that understanding, and that peace which is love in its pure form. You love to reach out to other people in friendship, this is the basis of all life; giving your love unconditionally without needing reward. It is the fundamental rule of the one who would be first that he understands and accepts every man and woman. It is the crowning glory that teaches us that all men are equal.

January. 2002.

REACHING OUT
In the reaching out there is a purpose and in that purpose will come change. It is a simple process that when you are reaching out you are applying the mechanics of change to your mind and your heart and this will achieve the things that you require, When you are not reaching out you are not allowing the changes to begin.

February 2002.

BRIGHT ANGELS.
All about you there are bright angels willing you to come with them to the party, to appreciate the love which they bear for you and which you bear for mankind. For in your heart there is only good.

February. 2002.

(Angel. The ancient word for messenger.)

Kindred spirits walk the pathway with you and expect you to do your best.   March 2002.

KINDNESS

Good evening, we are with you. Learning to be human is learning to be kind, no matter what befalls you, no matter what ills or pain or suffering that you confront. Kindness is the most important attitude, it is a way of seeing the world which benefits other people and makes it easier to come to terms with whatever ails you. Your kindness is without doubt, a feature of your personality, your generosity of spirit. And if you are to overcome your bitterness at those who would harm you (*harm others I'm thinking*) Both! You must remember that feeling of kindness, make it centre stage, return to it again and again until it becomes prominent and takes over your thinking. For kindness is always there in the back ground and people do evil things. They have a long road to travel, a road of regret, of doubt of wandering in the wilderness. It is then easier to be kind than judgemental for while they are in the throes of their thoughtless actions, careless words and deeds, this is the greatest test to another who has to allow them the latitude to learn, to experience and to overcome. When they hurt others they hurt themselves and when that period is over they will suffer pangs of regret. They will dislike themselves and distrust and destroy that which is good within them and then must then fight against that frame of mind, that state of mind and return to brighter pastures. Your world has stayed the same for a long time there have been no wars, no real hardships and no famines but that is about to change as your friends and relatives are drawn into the frame of mind which is of revenge and distrust of their leaders. And in coming to these conclusions they desire change which is not always beneficial and so the turmoil begins. See how easily peace is destroyed when people disagree. But strengthen your mind, against these things; leave them for other people to worry about whose lot it is to sort them out. You can do nothing but support the worthy, the good, the well meaning and appreciate that those whom you call bad are having a period of regression. They storm the battlements, they make war, they agitate, they cry out but they are not thinking people they are acting out the scenario which has been growing in their minds (or) planted in their minds by circumstances, by others who are vengeful who see their world as a place of conflict brought about by others who they would dearly like to kill. Take hold of the baton we give you; make your mind up to be light and airy; friendly; conciliatory; delightful and kind. Put before you the glory of God; His presence within you. His knowledge and His love will protect you and help you through and settle your mind. The story of your life is a creative one it has brought you many thoughts many ideas many considerations. And these are all valuable to your progress for without experience you cannot be wise, without knowledge you cannot understand. Learning to live is an awesome task but special times compensate and love brings wonderful things, to lighten the load. When day is done and you have settled down think only of God, of the wonders of heaven, of the special people who guide you, the mums and dads, the brothers and sisters, the cousins and aunts and uncles – and uncle Tom Cobley and all. For their task is to bring light into the world from which they have recently left. Their understanding is great because of their recent experience and their desire to help makes them ideal to take on some of the challenges of their wards. Allowing them into your life makes you a wiser person, helps you and helps them as they exchange ideas put forward new thoughts. They read you the riot act, calm your fevered brow and settle you down for the night. Over the way there are many voices calling imploring you to begin in earnest, begin the journey. Strengthen your will to be determined. Brow beat yourself no longer. Heaven is where the heart is and love is all around. Make peace with yourself. 26th June 2014

HEAVEN ON EARTH.
Create for yourself a heaven on earth: A mindset that says you can and you will, that appreciates the things about life that give it shape and form; the precious moments; the loving faces that surround you and the willing hearts. Christ is with you, you must appreciate this, you are never alone; you are filled with light and yet you know it not. February. 2002.

INJUSTICE.
Yes please begin. In the way that you approach the problem of injustice you are confrontational and dismissive of other people's ideas. - Things are never quite as simple as they seem. You must accept that there are things un-revealed that you are not privy to and that change the picture. In the feelings that you get of injustice there is that germ of honesty and justice however because it is unjust that does not mean that you should heap upon it more injustice by attacking those who you see to be in error. They have their way of thinking and it is for them to learn that there are other ways of thinking. Without this phase of experimenting by looking for conclusions, none of us would learn, everyone would have the same opinion; it is not a realistic or practical idea. People must make mistakes and yes other people must suffer because of that. But when these mistakes are rectified and everybody moves on a great deal has been learned and everyone is happy again. Take away the imperfections and you take away the lessons. You spoil the chances of anyone ever understanding what the real issues are and that is coming to terms with differences, learning to live with them till one day those differences are resolved. If everybody confronted everybody else who had a different belief it

would not be possible to live on this earth without constant conflict. From us to you Goodnight, God bless. March. 2002.

Good evening. Give yourself the opportunity to redress the balance within your own being the terms of your commitment mean that you are very heavily biased towards how things should be in your view, whilst failing to understand the causes and effects that apply in any particular case. None of us are perfect, all of us have to learn therefore when someone is a victim of injustice it means that someone has a lot to learn. And whilst you can blame them to a certain extent much of the blame often lies outside that person's control in another sphere of influence where the individual is helpless to change the tide of events. This we feel is the most frustrating situation, to encounter first hand injustice so if you are distraught imagine how these people feel. Sometimes in the past we ourselves have inflicted injustice upon others and have had to come for forgiveness or understanding, not least from our own selves and now, when other people are making mistakes you must learn to accept it as part of the pattern of life that ebbs and flows, sometimes in a person's favour sometimes against. But always there is a sense of purpose for when people are unjustly accused they are learning something that might help them when the situation is reversed. All of us have to be a victim, all of us have to be a perpetrator, and so it goes and if you are looking for perfection in this world, if you are looking for justice, then you fail to understand that justice returns to Him who gave it and that in all worlds, in all universes justice prevails in the long run so while you might feel distraught at this point in time a wider view of things would show you that everything is accounted for, the books are always balanced, and I repeat, everything returns to Him who gave it. March 2003.

DESPAIR.

Never again will you judge those who cannot fend for themselves, who may seem to be lesser mortals, hedged about by weaknesses and frailties that might seem to you to be of their own making. You now understand how a thought can grow and become unmanageable, how it can become difficult to deal with, to push to one side, because it grows bigger than it's creator and the force with which it moves is the force that has been put into it over a long period of time: A formidable force that can remove the will to resist, that can make the sufferer powerless and impotent. And so thoughts that are in their embryonic stage; that are played with; toyed with; and entertained, must be put in their place before they grow too large and unmanageable. Seek always a peaceful mind. Brush aside the thoughts of the negative, enjoy the moment, entertain thoughts that are wise and good and take only the steps that will take you upwards and outwards rather than downwards and inwards. October 2002.

GOING HIGHER.

The purpose for my speaking tonight is to encourage you to look within towards that light which is given to all mankind; to encourage and kindle it; to express it; to allow it to grow; to be fruitful and to listen for a higher order of thought with which to be at one with the higher forces. Expect the best for yourself and the best will be given. Teach yourself to elevate your mind; bring it into your daily life and make it a habit to express your thoughts in a manner that is worthy of you, which is spiritual. Sometimes there is a great awareness within you of that, which is possible, and yet you are inclined not to reach out for it and to let it lie fallow, to be content with things as they are. It requires from you a little effort, a little encouragement in order to allow it to grow and to fulfil the best within yourself. It is for you to initiate the longing and the desire to elevate your mind and it is for you to ask for that help in order that you might do so.　　　January. 1992.

GOD'S LOVE.

Good evening. Look for your way forward. God is with you constantly; your guide and mentor, protecting you; helping you through all the facets (or phases) of your life; teaching you; correcting you; scolding you; admonishing you; loving you; caressing you. In His mind he gently holds you, an object of His love, a precious thing; He wishes only the best for you. He takes you by the hand and leads you through life into a pattern of experience, of wonder and enchantment, of hardship and difficulty. Each a contrast with the other, always this ever changing pattern is feeding our soul creating within us a being of splendour and beauty and fashioning out of clay a wondrous thing to behold. Then when he has created you in His image it will be your turn to work with someone who needs your help and guidance, who looks to you for comfort and succour who asks you things that you cannot give because to give them would be to take away the opportunity to grow, and to understand those deeper issues. In all of our lives we have this ever-changing situation that brings us the richness that we call living, in order that we might understand that which has gone before and that which will follow. When life is over on the earth plane then you will be able to measure just how much you have grown. You will see the value of the hardship you have suffered; you will experience the rewards of the things you have done to help others and the pain of those things that have hindered them. This too will be a time of growth and understanding and it has been given to you to experience this particular pathway that you might grow in understanding, that you might help others on the way, that you might fulfil those things those tasks that you set out to learn by experiencing those happenings. By coming to terms with those problems and difficulties and the reality of being on earth which is not being in full control of the circumstances that surround you, it is time to put to bed thoughts of a magical existence where everything works out in your favour and accept that the spiritual holds the key to the real meaning, the pattern of our lives and that whilst we may believe that we have been unlucky there is really a hidden agenda that is shaping and moulding the way you think, the way you react, what you believe and how you will grow both in the next phase and beyond. December 2002.

THINK POSITIVE.

Expel the negative, anticipate the positive, and free yourself from the shackles of the material world. Come with us in to the spiritual light that will illuminate everything that you do. It is for you to make the effort it is for us to guide you, to help you to fortify you; this we cannot do without the initial effort from you without the desire to go forward. There can be no easy fixes in spirit, there must be periods of trial, of coming to terms with the shifts in viewpoint, with the things that try your patience and take your mind away from the spiritual path. Fix your mind on the stars; endeavour to let them be your guide. - To find brightness in the darkest night to find hope in the most hopeless situations and all the while keeping merry as you go along your way; freeing your self from all the things that have pinned you down and held you hostage. November 2,000.

THE WORLD.

Love created the world that we might learn, that we might understand, that we might experience the pains and the passions of being human. In our world there is an absence of this kind of pressure, in your world there is much to occupy your mind, to challenge your soul, to bring you that understanding that only the human body can bring. In time you will realise that while you are on earth there are a great many souls working with you and through you and helping you with their goodness and their concern: Helping you to meet your goals; inspiring you and directing you. In the fullness of time you will understand what those goals were, what they meant to you and how important it was that you understood them for when you created them you did have in mind certain lessons, certain aims and objectives. There were promises; unfulfilled; heartaches never reconciled; suffering not come to terms with, and a myriad other things so when you did elect to come back to earth you did have certain goals in mind. As earth is a meeting ground for many different minds it was inevitable that you would interact with others who had different lessons to learn, who had different objectives, many of whom had forgotten their promises and many of whom still had a lot to learn. And so when you think about the world, and all the troubles in it, when you ponder on the meaning of suffering and evil, remember this: Wherever there is evil there is good. Because in order to see the evil it has to be contrasted with good (*Like light and shadow*.) At the end of a life there are many things to consider, how much it affected other people, whether it had a positive effect or a negative effect, how many people were helped and how many people were hindered. In this world we see clearly the motives and the ambitions that you have in your minds, in your world you are not even able to see your own motives. For how many people tell themselves lies and make excuses that they might do what they want to do without fear of retribution or criticism. In our world we see clearly and everything that we have said and done is seen in its true light. Love greets you and takes you forward and shows you the way as it has always done. And as you consider the life you have lived it is then that you understand the true purpose of the world and the part that you played in its making. Love will bring you all of the things that you feel are necessary for your own progress in the future.

March 2003.

THE WILL OF GOD.

I come to you in the name of the Lord: That is the Lord of all that is, that created the Universe; who is at the centre of all; that knows all sees all, and understands all. God is with you every step of the way. It is He who draws the final curtain; He it is who opens the door to life and it is through His will that we have the experiences that lead us forward. God teaches you, tries you, and tests you: He turns you around and helps you to look at things from different angles. He makes things possible that seem impossible. He alters that which is, so that that which helps is more useful, and that which deters, is cast aside. It is His to give and His to take away, and all through life we are at His mercy. (*I didn't like the tone of that*) All over the world, there are people praying to God, not being sure that He exists, not understanding their own position in the world, not being really sure of where they aught to be or what they aught to do. And God rules in a mysterious manner that He might bring His children out of the fire and into the light.

April. 2003.

LOVE IS ALL AROUND

Love is all around you, supporting you, guiding you, enhancing your positive thoughts. Your friends mingle with your day-to-day activities that you might learn from them and that they might learn from you to meet life's challenges, to enhance the positive, and reject the negative. Love is all around at all times, all we have to do is learn to be aware of it and as your friends come to you they bring their love also, that they might help you throughout the day. Everyone has their challenges, you call them obstacles, we see them as stepping stones on the road to progress, and we see challenge as an opportunity to grow, to be better than you were, to help yourself to help others. And this is the key to the richness of living for in helping others you help yourself, in loving others you learn to love yourself. And in keeping faith with the commandments, with the things that you have been taught, you learn to discipline your minds, to follow the golden rules, to get the best out of your lives on earth. As helpers and guides we have to struggle just as much as you do with our emotions, with your emotions, with your attitudes and we also have to learn that in the flow of things there is a richness which tends to be forgotten by most people as they concentrate on their goals. We want you to be aware of this richness, of this love that surrounds you, to allow it to enhance your life and with that the lives of others, and as we see you grow, we love you more than ever and look forward to a happy and fruitful life for you and your friends. God is watching over all of us. God bless. May 2003.

PEOPLE.
Peace be with you. Of all the things in the world that are the most important people and their individuality are without doubt the pinnacle of creation. Their love; their hates; their desires; their experience; their troubles and their motivations: These are the things that are of the most concern to those who work in spirit. Of all the issues in all the world individuals are at the heart of every scenario: how they react, how they keep themselves together, or pull themselves round, or beat the odds, or keep a clear conscience, or fall prey to their own weakness. It is a complicated subject but it is what life is all about: Learning to avoid the traps, the pitfalls, the mistakes and the misunderstandings and being able to overcome them; to rise like a phoenix out of the ashes and reach for something much better. Looking for the good in all things makes the individual more positive, more grateful and more understanding of what this great Universe is all about. Being able to accept that which is termed bad along with the good is a sign of maturity, of understanding that things are as

they are because there is no other way. To form an opinion you must have understanding, to have understanding you must experience both sides of the argument. To experience both sides of the argument you must suffer and be able to know at first hand what the other side of the coin is. We come to you in order that we might help, that we might coax you out of the gloom, that we might tempt you into the sunlight, that we might take your hand and lead you forward (into the promised land) And when we come to you we learn to understand how you think; what makes you tick; why you do what you do and why you do not choose to do certain other things. In your mind we see the desire to do good; to make everything right in the world; to overcome obstacles and to reach out for something better. In your actions we see that you are reticent, unable to push yourself forward and desiring to stand on the sidelines. And so we have to convince you that what you know is good, is worth following even if it brings discomfort and unhappiness because everything that we do teaches us; brings us knowledge; makes us stronger; enables us to climb higher and in climbing higher we see more clearly. The things that used to upset us, the troubles, we put them in their place and we are more calm and serene, our hearts are filled with love, our minds are peaceful, and we know these things will pass as quickly as they came. But for someone who is new to the world these things seem very traumatic, very troublesome and overpowering. But as they go on they are able to accept more and put things in their place along side the vast array of happenings that join end to end throughout a life. The way forward is clear, take the pathway ahead of you. (*Phone rings.*) We come to you hoping that you will pick up the threads of our conversation. We try to impress you with ideas, hope for the future and fortitude, bringing you the threads of our thoughts. Over the way many voices are calling, keeping you on the straight and narrow, supporting you and trying to create for you an environment that will help you blossom; nurturing you; sorting out your thoughts and trying to coax you forward. When the time comes for you to pass over you will want to be able to say that you have put your house in order. It is now time to clear out the attic of your mind, to see things in a better light, to correct the errors in your thinking and to look forward to better things as a matter of habit. Taking your mind into a new framework that does not dwell on the negative but which is constructive; which is creative; which makes you feel that your life is worthwhile and that you are of value to others. Sorting out your mind is a priority, a fundamental thing that most of us never get around to but something which is essential to your welfare and your future in the spirit world where mind is so important (*all embracing?*) The seasons of your life fluctuate and when you create for yourself a harbour of refuge where you can seek shelter from the storm this enables you to be strong and to be ready for the next test or trial.

THE GIFT OF LOVE
Life is being very kind to you, learn to trust it. Try to appreciate that which life brings you for you have the gift of love which transcends all barriers, all creeds and denominations and forges a bond with your fellow human beings who wait, who cry out for knowledge and understanding and need to know that they are loved and valued as much as anyone else in the world. The poor believe themselves to be forgotten, we know that they have their place at the table along with everybody else. Make it known to them, speak to them, and make it as true for them as it is for you. Close the door now. God bless.

LOOKING BACK.
When you reach the world of spirit, and as you stand and look back over the years, as you join with one another and reflect upon the things you have said and done, and the bitter

battles you fought with one another, you will laugh heartily for you will see that the real meaning of all of this was to teach you to love one another, to care for one another and those with whom you have fought your bitterest battles will perhaps become your dearest friends. June 1991.

THE MIND.

Good evening. God wishes to come into the hearts and minds of His children; to make them aware of His presence; to be with them in their hour of need; to help them understand that which they are going through; that which troubles them. We are His messengers, we come to your side in order that His words might be heard, that they might be shouted from the roof tops for all to hear. Love brings many into the fold that they might shelter from the storm that they might have respite and that they might be able to come to terms with that which troubles them. Also to help them learn to understand the meaning of their lives and in so doing meet the challenges more fully, more competently with a good heart with a brave heart with an anticipation that good will triumph, that everything will be equal in the end. We, who come to guide you, learn just as you learn. We suffer as you suffer; we have our anxieties and our concerns. But we have that inner knowledge we have that added strength and the presence of God which helps us and strengthens us as we deal with the issues that we have been sent to help with. When we come into the world of man we are aware of a great many things. In this sea of minds we feel the pull of our old selves, as we once were, with our failings, our weakness our inclinations and we have to be strong and resolute in order that we might bring you something of that strength of character that helps us overcome these weaknesses. We come into your lives in order that we might teach what we were taught and learn as you will learn. That the human mind is a wonderful thing but it's vagaries are a challenge to the spirit; an opportunity to progress; a great gift from God that we must learn to treasure, that we must learn to understand, that we must learn to control. For the mind is an expression of that which is at our inner core, our inner being and whilst it represents many things, experiences through which we have been, it needs to be disciplined, it need to be kept in check. When the day comes that we pass over we will understand how important it was that that which has been our companion along the road and a part of our very personality, must be controlled and disciplined and not allowed to dominate or detract from our central goal which is that peace with God. All over the world people are calling needing a glimmer; a sign; the hope fulfilled that God is; that He is with them in their hour of need; that He will look after them and be with them always. And as they search desperately for signs of His influence they are unable to see that which is before their eyes; that which God has given the world to demonstrate His presence, to make it clear that His love surrounds each and every one of us. Over the way many voices are calling to mankind asking him to follow the path of light, to look into their inner being for the answer to that which troubles them, to recognise that in the world of man there are false Gods and false promises whereas in the world of spirit there is only truth and hope and understanding. Love greets you, puts you on a pedestal and asks you to be kind to yourself. The way is clear. Opportunities abound, everyone is cheering you on. September 2003.

The mind is a strange thing, it takes you on many journeys, it pulls you in different directions, it dictates it's wants and it's desires, it allows you to see things in a different light, and just when you think you have the answer, it has tricked you, it has distorted your view of things and prevented you from seeing what is there. So when you think, think of things as they are think not of high-flown theories, but rather simplicity and beauty. June 2003.

OF HEAVENS AND HELLS.

Good evening. A blessing on you all. Yes, the far reaches of the human mind are indeed strange quarters. The thoughts you have belie your very deep seated beliefs. They bubble to the surface and in anxiety and worry become manifest as physical feelings. The cares you have, the feelings, are manifestations of the far reaches of your own mind. Control them and you control yourself. The scene which is set before you is being shaped and moulded throughout your life. It is for you to conquer, to come to terms with, to appease, to shape and to mould: It is yours and yours alone. The feelings you have, the negative and the positive all stem from your outlook on life, your thinking and your attitude, and if you are to succeed spiritually then you must examine and set to right that which is wrong. You must throw away unnecessary burdens, forget things which you can do nothing about and concentrate your mind on the positive. You exist only to see and observe; to fulfil that which is given to you; to expect nothing and to give all and this is true service. There can only be one way forward in the light of the spiritual and this demands that you follow procedure, that you take up your cross and walk with it and as you do so it will become lighter, it will be as if it does not exist. But allow it to burden your mind and it will, it will; it will become heavier. And so it is a strange paradox that your burdens become lighter when you attempt to carry them and heavier when you set them at rest. Take from me the help I have to offer. The strange world of the mind is the world in which everybody dwells is the fount of all feeling, all knowledge, and all ignorance. There in the depths of your mind lie the heavens and the hells and it is for you to direct yourself towards the light, to live in heaven and to share your heaven with those around you.

"Come to me all who are heavily laden,"- Thus says the Master and in saying this He wants you to be one with Him in His mission, in His thoughts, in His prayers. Take my humble words and address them to your own problems. Seek and ye shall find, put right within you that which troubles you and you shall see. There will be a new dawn, a new beginning, a new horizon and new opening and you will experience a recharge, a new lease of life which will set you on the right path. It is for you to try and for us to support you in your efforts. Keep going, keep going on. Thank you for your love and your friendship. God bless. August 1994.

LOVE IN THE AFTERLIFE.

Tonight I wish to talk about love in the afterlife where it is natural to feel an at onement with others. We have our special way of showing love, of giving and receiving and it is a wonderful experience. Tonight I wish to talk about creating that sense of love where before there was nothing: Love grows through sharing and caring for each other; it is intrinsically bound up with our needs and necessities, our wants and desires. All are interwoven that they become part of our fabric, part of who we are and when we love one another we are in a sense loving a part of ourselves, that which is a part of our experience, that which we care for. And loving others enables us to move outside ourselves, to be less selfish to be more understanding, more forgiving, more accepting. When that love is for a while broken by separation, it grows and it matures for where there was a familiarity there was often misunderstanding and with separation there comes deeper appreciation of the qualities of love. No strings attached; no qualifications; blind acceptance of each other; warts-and-all; despite the differences and sometimes because of them. For in each other we see echoes of that which is in ourselves: That which is the basis of attraction is recognising the similarities, the harmony, the intunement of two souls who give to each other those special qualities that sometimes the other lacks or that sometimes the other shares. You my friend have love for strangers, people you have never met. You care about people, you wish them well, and you hope for their improvement and wish to help. Many people cannot see beyond their own needs but when that time comes for you to meet them face to face it is then that you are tested, your reality is very different from imagination. When you see for yourself the kernel of that person, what is at the core of their being, then you will understand how truly blessed you are to be able to accept that which is not obvious, that which is hidden. Christ is with you. His sermon on the mount is important, is worthy of consideration, and when all peoples can take these teachings and live by them, then the world will truly be blessed.

April 2003.

When two people love each other, they are prepared to make sacrifices, to try to understand each other, to give each other some latitude: Naturally they hope that their love will go on forever. In the fullness of time the experiences of life teach them new things about each other, they begin to see each other in a different light. Sometimes this is challenging, even threatening to a relationship and great efforts must be made to overcome the differences, the misunderstandings, and the alteration in viewpoint. Out of that can grow a new kind of love, a love that is less selfish, more about the other person, and more enduring. When the two people who began in such a loving fashion, spend their last years together, it is a different kind of love. This is not always obvious and only when there is separation do some people realise how powerful that love was, only when they are separated does that love come back in full force. And so the essence of love is endurance, perseverance, caring, sharing, making allowances and making amends. All kinds of things contribute to that special feeling which binds two people together. In your world there is much hate and rivalry and the power of love is often overlooked, as it is not obvious and only present when it is threatened.

SEPARATION

In every life there is a purpose and that purpose is to come nearer to God. Through each other we learn about ourselves, we learn to understand ourselves, and other people. And when at the end we are separated we understand as we have never understood before, the frailties, the faults and the imperfections. How often those faults and imperfections are at the very core of the one we loved and how part of the charm and the uniqueness of that individual made us love them so. And so when we talk of love we can talk of a temporary state of mind but in reality it is more enduring than that. It is ever present, all-powerful and all knowing for it is the very essence of the Father who created all and sees in our hearts the real truth of who we are, how we think, and how we relate to one another. *July 2003.*

THE GREATEST POWER IN THE UNIVERSE.

Love is the greatest power in the Universe. It pervades all space, enters into all minds, receives and entertains all souls and in its bounteous goodness, considers all people and all thoughts. All expressions of service and love find their way into the heart of this wondrous being: The service you give, the love you give, the comradeship, the caring and the sharing, all find their way into this treasure house of love. Tonight I want to give you inspiration to uplift you, to fortify you, to serve you. In His name I come that you might understand His purpose for you. With love He brings you gifts, with love He sees into your hearts and considers what He finds there; the riches and the treasures which you have built up over your lifetime: The service and the good deeds, the consideration and the kind thoughts, all these are contained in your storehouse. The treasures; the special moments; being together, sharing and giving; many different things which are like tinsel on a Christmas tree. Like the ornaments that shine brightly and glow, and bring you pleasures, they will return one day to delight you, to fill your mind full of joy, to bring you ecstasy that the life you have lived was so fruitful. And so consider friends that when you do a kind deed, give a kind word, you are adding to your treasures, you are storing your wealth, that you are giving something to that Universal storehouse of love. The knowledge you have is minimal and yet a great deal more than many of the people have on this earth. To you we look to introduce into the world wherever you can, knowledge of love, and an insight into the workings of spirit and in giving a service proving that spirit is alive and vibrant. I have many words to give you friends but my instrument is not capable never-the-less you catch my meaning. The service you give is a wondrous thing for even in the smallest measure it will be rewarded and will bring you pleasure in years to come. The life you live is full of contrasts and when you lighten the highlights you throw the events of your life into stronger contrast and so you suffer more greatly when you see injustice and pain because of the light within you. You see the contrast, you understand more fully and yet you are truly blessed because of your sympathy and your love, your outpourings, you are a greater soul. You are stronger and more prepared to take your place with the angels. It is for you I bring my message of love, to share with you, to share with your company of friends and I bring you my best wishes and theirs too. God Bless. **December 1994.**

POSITIVE THOUGHTS.

We entreat you to be careful of your thoughts, lift them higher. Turn the tide of events in your own life by anticipating good things, by hoping for a bright future; by building in your mind something which is optimistic and hopeful and ambitious. For there is nothing wrong with ambition when it is in the spiritual sense, you have many gifts to give, many hopes to fulfil. Be positive, be extra specially careful of your thoughts that they do not dwell upon stagnant ponds but dance like a butterfly over and above the troubles which you perceive and which you magnify out of all proportion. Pleasant times are coming, times when you will be proud of your efforts when you will have happiness in abundance, when you will see the fruits of your work. Tell yourself that these things will be, determine that you will do your best and set yourself upon the right road. Speeding along on the highway is all right but there are times when you must linger awhile in the bushes before you have the true perspective of the things around you and so go on, be of good cheer, full of hope and happiness. You have friends here who can give you all that you need; you only have to call upon them. First let me tell you a story: -.

LOOK FOR THE MASTER IN ALL THINGS

There once was a wise old man who waited everyday on a hilltop that he might see the Christ coming in all His glory. When the time came for him to leave his earthly body he became filled with light. His face beheld a countenance that was of great joy and happiness. Those who did not understand said that he had waited in vain whilst others knew the true meaning of that union with Christ. But let me tell you there is no need to wait on a hilltop for His coming for He is here now in you and you must learn to blend your thoughts with His, to be His servant, to be His companion, to be His child. You must see in others the love He has for you. Guard your words well, be a different person in your demeanour, in your outlook and let your optimism shine through so that those who live with you can feel the rays of warmth rather than the chill wind of pessimism. Spend your time on these things and it will be well spent. The effort you make now will be repaid a thousand fold, let me assure you. Look for the Master in all things. He it is who rules the world and takes account of your feelings, who puts right what is wrong, who guards and guides you but He can do no more than lead you forward. It is not for Him to do your thinking for you, nor to take you out of the world in which you live, but He will strengthen your resolve and help you overcome the obstacles that stand in your way. These for you are obstacles of self rather than those of worldly conditions

HOPES AND DREAMS.

It is in the dreaming that will make things come true for without our dreams, without our imagination where would we be. We would be an empty void, a mechanical man with a sameness, a concreteness, unbending and inflexible and when our lives were over they would all have been the same. So forge ahead in your own unique way, only you can do it. Forget the trials of the past and look forward to the future in eager anticipation spending your time working for God and doing the things that He would have you do in the service of others. 'Climb every mountain, ford every stream; follow every rainbow, till you find your dream.'

THE NEW YEAR.

Tonight I wish to speak about the coming year: its expectations, the problems that will come and go, the hopes and the heartaches and the harmony that are all part of the pattern of living. And I want to set the scene for a brighter future, an elevated future: a scene that is full of anticipation and hope. All of the workers are refreshed and come in great power to help you through a new phase of life in anticipation of good things to come. They expect the best for you and only the best will satisfy them, and if we can be of like mind, then we can profit by one another's company. In the future you will see new horizons, your expectations will increase and you will not be disappointed. There is much work to be done in the spiritual sense and that work begins with the self.

In expecting the best for yourselves you motivate and you create the power that will urge you on, that will reach out into the world unseen and which will help you to form the basis on which to build your spiritual home. There are many about you that will tell you a different tale of their lifetime, of their hardships and of their experiences, and all come to you with hindsight, with greater wisdom than when they lived on earth. They hope to enthuse you with something of that energy with which they now feel the joy of living: that purposefulness, so that you might take from them something that will aid you in your travels. The very essence of living is harmony, is the love of life, and is the creation of new thought patterns and the coming to terms with old ones. And so as you go into the New Year I want you to dispense with all that lies heavily upon your mind. I want you to take a new look at yourself, a new leaf from the book, to expect something refreshing, something new. Something that will help you to feel that life has more to offer; that you are learning and that you are turning to a new chapter in the book. This visualisation will all help you to strengthen your position and to go forward. The very air you breath is of the very essence of the Father, He never leaves you. Always someone is aware of your innermost thoughts, always there is someone to guide and to help and to protect you. But there is always an obligation to return that love and that kindness and so we hope that you will always remember those who work with you unseen, and in that moment of stress, of pain and sorrow and of anxiety, to draw strength and comfort from that knowledge and those about you will gladly come in response to your thoughts.

Each day brings its problems; each day brings its joys, but set the scene within your own mind. Be prepared to accept the best and the best will come. For now I want you to draw strength and pleasure in the knowledge of those who love and surround you and I want you to take home with you a new

outlook, a new beginning, and a new way of looking at things. Prepare yourself; prepare to scale the heights in anticipation of better things. This is my wish for the New Year.
January 1992.

JESUS.

He was a leader of men, a great light in the world and His teachings are of the highest. He wishes it to be known that His love for mankind brings Him into close contact with many souls who are looking to Him for light.

In His lifetime He wished to open the gates of knowledge that many might pass through. He wanted so much to see the faces around Him bear an expression of hope and expectation instead of their over-burdened demeanour caused by the pressures which so many felt in their day-to-day living. He wanted to tell the truth, but how difficult that truth is to tell, simple though it may be. There are so many who would twist it and turn it and stand it on its head and it is not in the nature of things to be so simple. They always managed to accumulate lots of ideas that were not thought of in the beginning, which clouded the issue and caused misunderstanding to many-

His mission to earth was one of propagating truth and giving an insight into the spiritual life. His task was to follow the train of religious thought that had been prevalent hitherto and embellish it to give it new life, to bring new meaning into outworn, outmoded beliefs. And this he did; he injected into old ideas a new immediacy, a new feeling that was to ignite the spiritual essence of the listener that set a fire burning within their hearts and minds and which brought about a new wave of religious understanding. Prior to that time there were many good men but for the general population the message had lost its meaning and become stale and the way of approaching God was at a distance. It had not the sense of personal involvement that Jesus brought to His teaching that you were in a sense close to the Father and not at a great distance from some stern authoritarian God. It was a mission that succeeded in the main and which still has its effects on the world and there are ever growing numbers of people who are listening to His teachings.

There have been many who took this newfound religion and abused it: This is the resistance that is always set up to new ideas, a kind of backlash; and there are always individuals who will exploit any avenue they can to their own advantage.

He brought us to an understanding of ourselves, our way of life and of our Father that had not been present hitherto. In His mission to give knowledge to mankind, to bring them light, He taught that, to keep faith with God, and to keep faith with one's fellow man, was the prime commandment and was the most necessary action for those who were going to be successful in life.

He tried to bring this spiritual outlook to His followers. He was intent on making them all aware of the responsibilities which lay upon their shoulders: That this life is a testing ground; one which we undertake that we might examine our attitudes, that we might make progress and that we might overcome things which hold us back. His task was to enlighten those who were entrenched in religious ideas which were a deterrent to an enlightened mind and which were a bar to further progress. His purpose was to remove all obstacles so that those souls could fully understand the possibilities that lay before them. In time these stories became much simplified. His attempts to put the kernel of truth into a story that would carry on without distortion through many tellings were indeed successful and the message has reached, even unto this day, fairly intact. He was in His day a great light in the world because man looked for some sign from his God. He wished to have that closeness, that personal involvement that was not present in other men or forms that were of sculpture or of individuals who claimed kinship with their Gods and so when he came into the world they expected him to be in the manner of an earthly king. We know now that his mission was to bring spiritual truths into the world. Their anger when he turned away from their earthly ambitions was so great that His message was denied and many fell by the wayside. –

OF CHRISTIANITY

Forge ahead with your book, make it readable and make it presentable. *(I was concerned that this book would be equated with yet more unfounded religious ideas)* Forget terminology it will be read by people who can accept it. Make it plain that that is what you were given and not how you think. In your faith there is a great deal of love for those who guide you for the principles on which you stand, and the Master who is and was appointed to illuminate the minds of men. He hoped that his simple message would not be distorted or misused but the things that happened after he passed were in the hands of other people. They did not care or know what the true religion was and so they took it and used it in the way that they thought best. That way was to be over complicated, overbearing and not always in the spirit in which it was first conceived. However it has finally come into its own as a spiritual tool. More and more people are using it as a basis for something better; more congenial and more in keeping with the Master's original intentions.

I come to you in the name of the Lord. He it is who sees all things and knows all things. We know that you cry out for knowledge wanting to understand this or that but we tell you that it is not necessary for the ordinary person to understand the ins and outs of the world of spirit or even the world of man. To simply have faith that there is a greater power, a greater understanding is all that is really necessary. But you yourself are curious about these things, you wish to make them fit, you wish to put them together and build house which is strong and secure. But we tell you often it is a house of cards for without understanding without experience without being there to feel the reality for yourself you cannot really understand what fulfilment is. All of us are here wanting you to go forward, pick up the pieces and learn to accept what is. Open the door to graciousness: Be of good cheer, open the door and walk through into the light.

May 2012

OF OTHER LIVES.

We have told you of the journey through life, now we will talk of the journey through death: This is the turning point where man meets his maker. He takes time to reflect and sets off on a new journey reaching forth into the blue, determined that he will go forward into the realms above; and so he progresses and, as he progresses, he feels a certainty about his existence and overshadowing him is a mind which is telling him, that his individuality is but one of many selves. He will then become aware of those other facets of his being. He has many personalities and he looks with wonder at all of the things he has done, all the experiences he has had but it is tinged with regret when he sees that the same old patterns of life in which he has failed, have once again appeared in his most recent life: But there are no individuals to confront save those memories of his former self. They are not individuals in his own mind, but recollections of experiences, of journeys made through time and space in other worlds, in other places, in other states of being: and as he gathers them all together, and tries to make sense of them, he becomes more well rounded for he has more experience to add, a new point of view. And in examining his former selves he will discover that he has made progress, not necessarily in the things he desired but never-the-less, greater understanding of his former failures: a new and invigorating view of life for it has expanded so greatly from that narrow single existence of which he had previously been aware. If you wish to show yourself as a previous incarnation you can legitimately do so. You are not bound to appear as the person you once were and so when you are called upon by your previous family to return to their side you can do so, even though you may be born again. You have the memories, you have the facilities to appear as you once were, because this is you; this is another side of you; you as you once were therefore when you see your friends in the world of spirit making progress they are one but many. They are individuals, they are friends, they are comrades in arms, but they are also other people. They have within them the capacity to appear to others, as they would wish to. While they are with you they are your loved ones. While they are with others, they are theirs and so this multifaceted personality can, if it wishes, appear to others as they so desire, just as it appears to you and so my friend you see one of the mysteries of existence. These people you cling to in the world of spirit, your friends, your mother, and your father: they are but representatives of other souls, of other beings: they represent to you that which is different to others.

January 1998.

LOVE AND HATE.

Good evening. Love conquers all. Fill your heart with love and try to emulate the people that you admire. Bring into your mind things that will delight it, that will make you feel good, that will help you on your way. All that we can do is to support you in your efforts; there must be some input from your side. Love is the conquering hero and it is better that you love than hate for hate is a destructive quality that clouds the mind with frenzy and passion whilst love is a healing quality that picks up the pieces, that tends and cares for others. Love brings in its wake many good things; hate is destructive and knows no reason. It is a quality that is not beneficial to human beings. I am loving and kind in my outlook therefore I am creating a feeling of well being and meaning. To me the way forward is always positive. - What can I do to repair, to put right or to console, not to direct or domineer, to push or shove but to cajole, incline, and impress.

((*In my case its frustration – wanting to put the world to rights.*))

THE POOR.

(My thoughts.) We try to make the world a better place for the sake of our children not suspecting that we might also be doing it for ourselves. We are enthralled by Star Trek, by high technology and populating the planets never thinking that one day we might be taking part in that drama. Perhaps we ought to be considering how the life we are living now is shaping our life and maybe even our world the next time around in view of the possibility of coming back to earth again. If we do not improve the conditions of the poor and oppressed this time out of love and concern then perhaps we should do it to ensure that if one day we awaken to a new life such as theirs, things will be better because of our 'concern' last time around! I felt a lump in my throat when I heard the words of the 'Band Aid' tune which went,

'Thank God it's them instead of you.'

LOOKING FORWARD.
We have all come together that you might learn that you might open your heart to new things to new attitudes new hopes and new desires. That will entice you forward that will bring you out into the light that will give you hope aplenty and maybe, just maybe, will give you the will, to do the

things you want. I have just come from the spheres and have seen there the amount of suffering which still goes on for those who will not let go of their earthly ideas. It is for you to prepare yourself so that when you come to this side you are ready and able to accept a new pattern of thought without being enmeshed in the old one and to learn from your mistakes; to overcome them and to reach out for higher things. The principal idea of going forwards then is not to look back but to look to the future with an anticipation that things will go well, that you will achieve your goals, that everything will fall into place and if things then are not as you expected there is nothing lost. If however you look at the future and think that you will never achieve your highest aims and goals then you will not even begin to set about achieving them.

OUR SPECIAL CHALLENGE.

Good evening. Love is all around; helping you throughout the days; giving you strength; making you aware of your spiritual self; teaching you and helping you to reach out to that which will help you through life: A sense of purpose; a sense of hope; a sense of anticipation and of overcoming; being able to see the good in the bad and being able to meet the challenges. In every lifetime there is a particular challenge: Something which needs to be overcome, to be understood, to be grappled with, something which was meant to teach you, a special lesson. Whatever that test is it comes in different forms and only when we reach the world of spirit will we be able to look back and see that that was our mission in life, that was the thing that we were sent to achieve, to learn to come to terms with. And all the while lessons abound, there are so many things we need to understand, not least of all, ourselves and our fellow man. In learning about these simple things we find that peace; that tranquillity and that overview of human life that makes us free that allows us to accept people as they are without being judgemental, which allows us to accept ourselves as we are, without being too harsh. And as we learn to grow in peace and tranquillity so we are more able to give that to others, to instil within them that same sense of peace and security, that same sense of purpose. As we come to you in your circle we feel the love that abounds in the community of man and in the community of spirits. We pray dearly that you yourselves will have that pleasure and knowledge to help you throughout the days, knowing that we are always there, helping and guiding, strengthening you, making you aware of the things you need to know and telling you where your next step lies. So in all of these things there is a beautiful light, that power of love, that desire to help one another, and see each other's point of view. Then, when your lives are over you will know that you have done your best and that the people you leave behind felt something of that love and concern that you had for them and that they had for you. I come in the name of the Lord. God bless. August 2003.

CAUSE AND EFFECT.
When somebody thinks about their own position in life they imagine that they are invincible. That nothing bad will ever happen to them, that all the forces of nature will allow them to go by unnoticed and untroubled. In reality everything is working according to a plan. Evens are foreseen before they happen and then avoiding action can be taken where the prescription does not fit the illness. In the world of man there is a view that everything is as it is, that the forces of nature go on unchecked, that every time there is an accident there is cause and effect that is traceable to events in this world. In truth there are a great many influences that are brought to bear on physical manifestations in the world of man. In the tide of events we see that many are swept along by these mighty forces that seem to be out of our control. In reality

everything is foreseen and accounted for. At times it is a question of making the best of the events as they come towards us, triumphing over them or buckling down, being defeated or fighting back. Overcoming - taking stock, - assessing, - creating. - Action that may help us to avoid, actions that will help us to repair. Always something is gained from each event and if it is not quite as planned then it is always beneficial because all events in life teach us constantly. They test our mettle; they bring us blessings and create within us a strength of character and of thoughtfulness and knowledge. The mighty forces of nature are just one of many pressures and forces that mankind has to come to terms with. What I am illustrating is that within all of these seemingly uncontrollable forces there is a spiritual agenda, there has been an assessment made, the events have been looked over and where they do not fill the bill steps are taken to forge a new pathway that will be more suitable for the individual concerned. Love brings you greetings. Goodnight and God Bless. August 2003.

THE STREAM OF LIFE.

Life goes on its many ways, interminably it flows onwards throughout the centuries, each man playing his part, each contributing to the whole, day after day, year after year, century after century in a never ending stream going forwards and upwards. As mankind progresses he treats his neighbour in the same fashion as he would have him treat himself and so mankind learns to be more sensitive to the voice of the spirit within. But always there are contrasts, there are those who will take the other pathway and plunge downwards into the darkness of the soul. Always there are those who are a trial and a tribulation to those who would walk in the light and always there is this contrast, this frustration, this misunderstanding if you like. But there is a point to be made in all of this - that through these misunderstandings, through this friction, we learn to love one another, we learn to compensate, we learn to make allowances, we learn to live together, through thick and thin, through hardships through pain and strife, through all of these things and the never-ending stream continues and goes onwards into that distant future, which is with God. And as I tell you these things there are many who surround you, many great souls and many humble ones, all on different levels, all contributing towards the whole. - Great minds, wise minds, simple minds, loving minds. - So many souls contributing to that which we call life and so very happy to give their all to you in friendship, comradeship and love. And so you will be asked to do the same, to give selflessly, to give your all and to give that which you have that others might see something in their lives which is of purpose, which is of value. So many souls are wandering in the darkness, not understanding that there is a purpose for them, something that they can contribute and yes! something which they can take from life which they have not understood: Something which will give them a better quality of life which will help them through their difficulties. And all the while the voice of spirit continues trying to interest man in spiritual things, trying to instil within him the goodness and the simplicity of the life of the spirit. And as we come to you, and as we surround you with our love, and as we try to lift you onto a higher plane, all of us contribute something of our own inner self, something of that quality of life which we have learned, which we have gained through each step of the way and as we contribute so we are rewarded in the measure in which you take from us that knowledge and that love and pass it onto others. And when you do things for others you do things for us and you do things for the whole of the community and you add something of that lustre to the total brightness and so you contribute towards that which is good. You give of your best and you increase your radiance, your light, your love and your understanding and also your power: The great power which you hold and have built up through unselfish acts, through unselfish thoughts. And so it will continue and it will grow into a radiant light and then you will find yourself in the presence of those beings whom men have called Gods but who are simple souls that have followed the pathway of right and have gone on to reach the dizzy heights. And so friends my hope for you is that you will follow this pathway, for all is there to be gained and nothing to be lost for this life is a fruitful one if followed in the spirit. And if it seems a daunting task to you take the point of view that it is there as a right; there to be given to you; to be taken. And as we shower you with blessings; as the good God above gives all to you that you desire; all that you need for your progression; take it freely and willingly and share it with those around you. For then you will truly find the joy of living and when you reach the end of your days you will be glad of everything that you have experienced. And more so for the bad things, for the difficulties for they are the jewels in your crown. The love that surrounds you is limitless, it is beyond measure and this is the love that I send you tonight. God bless. October 1991.

SHARING KNOWLEDGE.
We ask that all of you should join together in hearts and minds that we should see the great light ahead, the great possibilities, the wonderful work which can be done. And that in patience and understanding you can bring yourselves into the fullness of spiritual light to share with us the love of God and His concern for His children. Come to us with arms open wide that we may join together in this wonderful work for where we can share together the joys of helping one another there we can truly say is the spirit of our Father. And it is He who inspires us to do this work that we may bring to you some of the nobility, some of the upliftment which is His mark, which is the sign of His presence. And in coming to you tonight I want you to understand that this work that you do in all honesty, and in truth, is dedicated that we might

bring to others the knowledge that their lives are worth living, that they have a purpose to fulfil: A destiny, that they too can share in the Love of the Father, that they can bring into their lives that rich essence of the spirit. And in giving you my words I am always conscious of my inability to express myself as I would really wish in order that I might bring you some knowledge of the grandeur of the scheme of things, to bring into your hearts and minds some of the riches of the spiritual life and of the purpose of the light which surrounds us all. And even as we speak there are many about you who have reached out into the higher spiritual realms, who have brought down to you something of their power and their knowledge and stand ready waiting so that you might partake of that knowledge and that love and that friendship that they have to offer. And as you progress, and as you grow, so you will feel that bond of love that is offered from the higher spiritual realms. And we who labour long and who tend your needs, and who help you to understand yourself, your own emotions and the emotions of others, we tell you that there are great things ahead for those who look to the spiritual life; there are riches untold and though they may be in spiritual terms they are never-the-less very real. We take our leave now and ask you always to remember that we are there and are always willing to share our love.   June 1989.

OPPOSITE POINTS OF VIEW.

In your heart you know many things, you are a good person and you wish only the best for people but in your mind you try to force people to think as you think, to see as you see, and to become what you are. If you create the right conditions then perhaps they will see your point of view but the forceful approach never works, it has always been a guarantee of rebuttal. When people are given thoughts they will accept them and ponder on them, when they are given strong words their intelligence is insulted and they resist.

THE MAKING OF A SOUL.
The time will come when you will look back with fondness on your lives, on the memories, the experiences, the hard times, the good times, all the things we shared together. As we look back from the world of spirit it seems but a dream, a passing fancy, in truth it was the making of a soul: The building blocks that go to fulfilling that dream and to experience that which is of the essence of life and of living itself: The different facets, the conclusions you come to, the decisions you take, the twists and turns, and more over the love you share together through your experiences. It grows steadily, though you are unaware of it, and only at a time of separation do you really understand what that love means to you. In coming to you tonight I want to share that experience which is the experience of those in spirit who have passed through the change called death, who have understood what separation means from both sides feeling the loss, the bereavement, and seeing those loved ones left behind who think you gone. They understand not that we are there standing by their side, as cheerful as ever, wanting to help and yet unable to make an impression.

And so we have seen things from both sides friends, we know what it's like and we can see the value of our lives as you cannot yet see. And we want you to take heart, to experience that uplift, that upturn while there is plenty of time. Perhaps if I were to tell you of the experiences of the many souls who arrive here in such a dishevelled state of confusion and disharmony then you will realise how important it is that we set the record straight before the time comes for your passing. It's important that you get your house in order and that you attempt to experience something of the spiritual right here and now. In our lives we were totally unaware and we plodded on, we took our experiences and we fought against the tide of events. But you are more fortunate, you can learn to ride the tide with freedom and take from it the strength you need and experience the richness that is all about you. Fear not for the future is bright in this work which is of God, which is for your fellow human beings, to bring together the two worlds in harmony: Something of the spiritual world into the human world that others might experience that uplift, that upturn. - It is there for all who seek it.

Clear your minds of all the debris; experience a new birth; forge ahead in your thinking. Allow yourselves to open the windows of your mind and let the light flood in. I have experienced that light: It is a wonder to behold. The great power it brings into your being is beyond expectation and if you can sample but a little of it now it will help you in your work, it will help you fight your battles, and it will enrich your lives. See how easy life flows when you follow the tide. God be with you. July 1991.

THE GOOD AND BEAUTIFUL

When you leave this earth you will look back upon a life of varied interests one which has been in the main good and kindly, but it would have been a lot easier had you been able to enjoy it to see the side of life that is so beautiful, that is creative, that is simple and yet profound. Your life has been spent anxiously waiting for bad news concerning yourself with what might go wrong, never accepting that the challenge is in bringing forth something beautiful from something that is not so beautiful. Challenges to you are an inconvenience, a curse, and a major source of irritation whilst challenges are to me an opportunity to shine, to overcome, and to meet the problem head on. In your life you have looked at the very fundamentals of existence and yet you have completely missed the point. There have been times when you have been told that this was so and yet you have not accepted that the way forward was to feel for the good and beautiful aspects of everyday life. February. 2002.

A SPIRITUAL QUEST.

And as I ask you to look to the spiritual life I ask you not to don sackcloth and ashes or to take up the religious life like a monk or a hermit, none of these things are necessary. It is simply a matter of allowing the power of love to illuminate your minds and your hearts to give you that strength and that purpose so that you might help others in a simple way and through this enjoy your lives. Enjoy the challenge of life; enjoy helping others and giving them that strength that they lack. Help them to see that love radiating from you that it might touch their souls, that you might be able to help them on the path of life, and in doing so strengthen your own soul. All of us are wont to weaknesses and temptations, that is understandable. God never judges us, He helps us kindly to see the results of our misdemeanours and our weaknesses and to take hold of the challenge and go forward. He never condemns, He looks with an understanding smile as we fail again and again and he stretches out His hand that we might take it and go forward once more to succeed where we have failed. And in succeeding and in growing we grow more in His likeness and we share together with one another that love which is of Him, that bountiful presence, that awesome power which rules the universe and yet which is ours, which knows the number of hairs on our head, which knows when a sparrow falls. The power of God, the greatest thing in life, in the Universe, is at our disposal, that we might reach out and feel His power, His love and that we might carry His message to the ends of the earth.

People, who say that these things are not necessary, that they will come in their own time, are deluded for what is life but a spiritual quest. Everything we say and do, the very ordinariness of it, our work, our play, and our families, are all part of that quest. So be not deceived, it is not something we can run away from, it is always there beckoning. It stands on our doorstep ready to be taken as a challenge and if we can direct our minds to the brightness, the brighter areas within, then we will feel that life is truly worth living. Be gone the misery and the depression, of looking into the dark areas searching for problems. Let go of these things and put your hand in the hand of that great power. Always there is someone who cares for you, always there are many friends and loved ones surrounding you, showing you the way forward, helping to guide you, helping you to make the right choices for all of life is a question of choices: Whether to choose the higher or the lower, for the bad or the good, whether to be selfish or unselfish. All these things and many more are part of the spiritual quest. And if you can learn to choose for right no matter how painful it may be; no matter how much you may begrudge it; no matter how much it is not welcomed by other people; if you can learn to do right and choose right then you will feel that stature; that growth of your soul; that strength which is of true happiness; that which is the true purpose of living; the spiritual life. And as I come to you with a simple message of hope and understanding and of love I hope you will take up the challenge and when you awake in the morning I hope that you will don your rose-coloured spectacles, I hope you will look to the world with brighter eyes and try to see the best in others and in yourself and in everything around you and try to live for the joy of the moment. That joy is in helping others, in unselfishly giving yourself for their benefit that they might see, that their souls might be touched by the message that you have to bring.

THE VOICE OF SPIRIT
All over the world the voice of spirit is calling to man to try to lift him out of his earthly roots and onto heavenly wing's. One day mankind will see the chances that he has missed but never fear, always there is the opportunity to go forward, always there is a new dawn, always there is a golden thread running through each life no matter how wasted you may think your life has been. Always there has been a purpose

and always you have achieved a great deal. Never fear that God is a harsh judge for he judges you not and one day you will see that the things you have counted unimportant will be like jewels in your crown and these are the times when you helped another without thought: You gave of yourself freely and you helped where it was needed.

VALUE EACH PASSING MOMENT.

Life goes on in the things that you do and it is imperative that you get the best out of it. Take your time to acknowledge what you are doing. Accept that the simple things each have their part in your life and that each moment is precious. If you wish to progress you must come to terms with every second as it passes allowing yourself the luxury of appreciating the passing of time, the inherent phases of life and the feelings that go with them. Only you can do this for yourself. When you have appreciated that which is small then you can enjoy that which is bigger. February. 2002.

TAKING STOCK

Taking stock of your life is never easy: you look back on your life and you feel that the years that have gone by have been wasted and that your hopes and glories never materialised. When you were a child you imagined many wonderful things and you went on undaunted on the path of life not caring for the morrow, not understanding about death, not being concerned whether it came or went but going forward and enjoying each day as it came. And as you grew older, as you took upon yourself the challenges of life, that simplicity of living was lost and the hardship and the heartaches crowded in until your mind became filled with the bitterness and the weariness of life but dear friends let it all go. It has been a hard taskmaster but has taught you a great deal. It has been of great benefit but let it go and reach out in simplicity for that which is of the spiritual and which is enduring and that which will bring you great honours when you reach the threshold of that new world. And when you look back along the years from this side you will see that there was a purpose for you and that everything you have said and done has brought you great benefits and aye, to those around you. For you have contributed in the making of the world no matter how humbly, you have progressed the cause of the earth and you have progressed the cause of spiritual truth for you have been good and true and honest and you have demonstrated to others the value of these things. In helping others we forget our own troubles and we find that which is the true purpose of all being. For mighty though God is and infinite in His wisdom, He helps you and me personally: He knows us by name for we are a part of Him and He a part of us and we are a part of each other. And all together we form that great and wonderful power which is unimaginable, which is limitless, which is great in its power of love. Tonight I wanted to paint a picture of enlightenment, something that will bring happiness to your step, which will make each new day a challenge but a challenge gladly accepted: Something which will bring a newness into your life; a refreshment; the wind of change; the hope for an opportunity; an opportunity to serve and to serve our Father God. For in everything you say and do that is the true purpose of living: To grow in His image, to go forward in His likeness and to reach out to Him that is the greatest power that we can ever imagine. I hear you say that this is very interesting, I see you forgetting. The words grow cold in your mind and as the week passes you are embroiled in the toil and the trouble of your daily life but dear friends give a moment of time each day to this thought: That the power of spirit can be yours; that there is a purpose for you and that purpose is a glorious one for it is growing in the image of God and in the image of those great lights who stand before you on the path of progression. And if you can take hold of this power then you will never look back and your life will be filled full of joy and upliftment. July 1991.

DIFFERENT PATHWAYS.

Love brings to each and every person special moments, insights, knowledge of where that individual is going and what he or she needs to achieve. Always there is an inner voice, teaching, guiding, and advising, it is up to the individual to choose to listen or to ignore. When each of us is at a cross roads we often hear the voice of reason telling us what to do, sometimes it may be something that we do not wish to hear but there is a debate which goes on within the mind to help crystallize that person's point of view, to help them to understand the true situation that the outcome depends very much upon other factors involved such as that person's inclination to go in a certain direction. The desire that may or may not be selfish, the pressure that may or may not be resisted, and a myriad other forces come into play to cause confusion and always there is the opportunity to choose right over wrong and good over bad. And every time that individual comes face to face with that choice he or she is given another opportunity to make a different decision, to take the higher path, to choose the better outcome and if he or she fails again, the experiences are repeated till that time that the right decision is made: It is then that the lesson has been learned and the final chapter written. After that a new direction is taken and different experiences follow and that process continues throughout all eternity that we might learn how to overcome that which challenges us but also how to listen to the voice within that tells us what we need to do and how we need to do it. And it is in the nature of things to work in that way by trial and error, the strong succeeding and the weak failing until each of us grows in stature and in power because of our experiences, because of our failures and in spite of them. Choosing the right path is never easy because it usually involves some sacrifice. Going forward is never easy because it requires (or demands) effort to change the status quo, to alter the frame of mind, to move on, to seek new pastures and to think new thoughts. Life allows us to move as we will; to choose, to make plans, to endeavour, to set forth upon our journey and to meet the challenges. When we fail we open up a different pathway, we move in a new direction and thereby learn that the way forward is the way that was meant to be: That which was meant to teach us to bring us knowledge of ourselves and our fellow man; to explore; to take upon ourselves new adventures and to meet the challenges head on. In these things the components, the ingredients, of our lives are mixed together as in a mixing bowl. We see a pattern that takes us by the hand through many twists and turns that we might understand and come to terms with all of the different facets of life.   September 2003.

BLOOD, SWEAT & TEARS.
Character building takes time and patience, one might also say blood sweat and tears, for through the trials and tribulations of life we begin to see things in a different light. We understand that which we didn't comprehend in the beginning and we overcome problems that at first seem daunting, that with hindsight were not so bad and in fact were often a good experience. Throughout life we are called upon to make many decisions, to overcome many obstacles, to fight many battles and to reach out to new ideals where the old ones have failed us. In accepting a new view of things our understanding deepens and we become more able to fight the battles that lie ahead. And though we may feel that life has dealt us a harsh hand, that things are not what we would like them to be, always we have learned, we have climbed the mountain of understanding and we look down from its lofty peaks to the time when we were but children: Then we saw things in a simplistic light. When we come to you we try our very best to help you understand that which is troubling your mind. We open our hearts to you, we share our

experiences with you and though you feel us not, though you hear us not, though you see us not, our thoughts are with you. Our love surrounds you, and our desire is for your welfare and for your growth in understanding that you might conquer the world of man in a spiritual sense, that you might grow in the image of God Himself and that you might take upon yourselves the mantle of love and harmony to enable you to win the battle. Love is with you. We will go now.

August 2003.

THE MANY WAYS OF LEARNING.
The Heaven of which you speak is with you now, round and about you, making inroads into your thinking, joining with you in impossible adventures. For the human mind knows no bounds, everything it wishes comes true if not in reality in then in dreams. Exploring the way out of trouble; seeing things realistically; opening doors in the mind and reaching out to other dimensions. All this it can do and more:- Sorting out your problems; giving you the agenda for the day; climbing ever nearer to God in your search for truth and wisdom and understanding. Little by little, step by step, you move nearer ever nearer to God. Everything you learn is precious, everything you understand is valuable. And even when you do not understand it is a marker; a pointer; a deal with destiny a recognition of something that needs to be understood; sorted; fixed and regenerated even. The God within you knows all hears all; sees all and feels all. It is not isolated as you are but far ranging. It reaches out to other souls to blend as one; to fix problems and to keep thinking. Opportunities abound because of this network of friends, even people you don't know coming together to make it happen. Love is always around you and about you fixing problems; inspiring; opening doors and reaching out to other people. The way forward is clear. Heaven is where the heart is. The underlying reasons for your life on earth act as a catalyst which will bring you into certain situations to meet

certain people to understand certain things. Nothing is left untouched; nothing is left not understood and all is included in this great plan that you might move forward in your own way in your own time but within these parameters that you might meet the objectives and go the mileage to reach the goal that you have set. 30th July 2015

THE FUTURE.

It is a strange fact that in looking towards the future we behold many scenes, many possibilities. We see activities that lead us to believe a certain thing will come to pass but this proves not to be and so in seeking to understand, to know what is in store for us, we must be aware of the pitfalls, the alternatives that are possible. In the higher realms of spirit we believe that all is foreseen, all is accounted for. In our world we are only dimly aware of the overall view and we work with that strain of thought that we are given. We are co-opted into the work and contribute whatever we can to its outcome. Naturally we hope for the best result from our point of view but always there is that wider view, that alternative view with a long-term benefit in sight that we cannot always see. That which happens in the short term may be a disaster but looked at in the long term may have results which were not anticipated, not foreseen by us and so these turn out to be blessings in disguise. People who tell the future are at risk of being involved in the wrong strain of thought and there can be mistakes made. When we tell you certain things are to come to pass we try most hard to be certain that they are true or we would not give you them. When you feel that we have let you down, perhaps it is the view that we gave which has become distorted in the telling and there has been a cross-purpose or a misunderstanding. Not everything goes according to plan in conveying our messages and so you must be aware of the alternatives and the conflicting points of view which may be presented to you, which may confuse you, and take account of them. Leave the future to those who can foresee it and be content with the present for it is with the present that we are concerned. February.1991.

THE GUIDES.

Try to envisage us in our spiritual garb as we surround you. Great lights come to you in love and serenity to calm your fevered brow, to express our thoughts through you in the hope that you will catch the flavour of something more spiritual. My friends are gathered here to impart to you some of their power and their wisdom and their love. It takes me a long time to enter into your world, to become one of you surrounded as I am by your thoughts and your feelings; immersed in your troubles, taking upon myself the cares of the world once more. As I come to you I must leave my home of rest where peace and harmony are the order of the day and be faced with a barrage of feelings, of expressions of doubt and all of the human failings and emotions. I must enter into your world once again and recall the thoughts I once had; seeing visions of past times, the battles I have won and lost, the glories which once were, and all of these things are as a sea before my eyes and I take from them the thoughts I want to express to bring to you something which is other worldly, that will try to lift you in a fashion out of your earthly thoughts and into heavenly realms. Difficult though it is I feel that it is worthwhile; I feel the power and the impetus that is given to me to do this work. And in keeping with my promise I return as often as I can to help wherever I can and those who work with me do so in their own way, their own fashion. I have many thoughts to give you my friends if only I could express them freely but it is not to be. I come to you in the knowledge that you will take the meaning of my words that you will make them yours and in your own lives, in your private world of thoughts I hope that you will come to us and visualise us as we stand in our spiritual glory and take that power from us of inspiration, of aspiration of elevation and of joy in another's face as they receive that knowledge, that comfort and that guidance that you have to give. I can only give you but dimly those thoughts that pass through my mind and I have much more to say but for now I will give you my love and send you the greetings from those who surround you. God bless. **August 1992.**

THE HELPERS.
Sometimes you are apt to forget that there are many spirit beings working on a particular problem. Where they can help they will providing their charges respond and if they can see the way forward and understand what needs to be done. But the world operates under its own steam; people are concentrating on their own lives; what they have to do; their daily duties; their interests; diversions from more serious matters; hoping for the best and working very hard. All of these things fill the mind and block out the influence of spirit who are trying to help improve the situation and move things forward. Until their charges can be cognoscente of a better way ahead they will remain where they are and sometimes stand in the way of progress. But their lives are mapped out that they might learn, come to understand and come to regret even so that when they pass over into our world they have learned a great deal about themselves and the world in which they live. And so it is with all of us nothing is ever wasted, there are wonderful opportunities to grow and to learn about new things: How to deal with people; how they think and where they are going wrong. The love that is within each of us binds together to brighten the world, to give it hope, that those who are in the depths of despair might see a glimmer of light; and those who have undergone great pain and suffering, will bounce back, re-charged and able to carry on but much more appreciative of the life they have lived.

March 2016

THE TIME IS NOW.
I ask you to remember that the opportunity is now, that you have so many years left on earth, only God knows how many, to make the best of them, to make them your brightest years, your happiest years. Though you may say to yourself yes but I have this problem, I am lonely, I have no money, and this is so difficult, try to be honest with yourself and ask God that you might understand your own problems, your own situation. Ask Him how you can come to terms with it, how you can make it a little brighter and how you can give to other people. Giving to others is the true essence of spirituality, as we give to others we feel something of the true purpose for which we were born: The Master taught us that; "Whosever would be the greatest must be the servant of all."
November 1989.

SLEEP.
The morning comes too soon when we must begin a new day with new hope, new vigour, new anxieties and doubts. It is a moment of awakening from a deep slumber during which the mind was set free and able to roam at will drinking in the sights and the sounds of the spiritual ready to return and face once more that which is part of our earthly life.
September 2003.

THINKING OF GOD.
When we think of God we raise our vibrations towards that which is of Him and this allows our spirit to be fortified and strengthened by moving away from things of a lower nature. Trying to absorb that goodness, that love, into your everyday life creates a sense of well-being and of purpose and of beauty in all around. Love in itself is a powerful force that can rule the senses and take over the mind in such a way that its benefits close the door to negative thoughts. And in these periods of enlightenment, of sensing that which is at the heart of creation, we are strengthened and made aware of the

possibilities within us that will allow us to reach out and touch other souls who need our help and require sustenance for their soul's understanding; for their minds; and love in their hearts. Christ came to earth that He might instruct those who would listen that if they would be of simple mind and of simple faith like little children, then they would understand something of the Kingdom of Heaven: That, that which was all around them, the mighty force of the God of love, would touch their hearts, would strengthen their minds and bring them the delights and the determination and the wonder of the world of spirit. And in being thus strengthened would allow them to love others unconditionally that they might see the true value of their lives in the spiritual, to love and to give unconditionally in the knowledge that this was God's work. That everyday was a bonus, an opportunity to make progress and to free themselves from that which is of earth, that which would drag them down, that which would ensnare their minds and cloud their judgement and depress their souls. That *is* the mission that we are engaged upon: To give that beacon of hope, of light, that others might draw comfort from it seeing it's light in the gloom and from that moment on begin to live as they have never lived before. In your world there are so many who simply exist not understanding nor caring why, not believing in anything outside themselves and all the while feeling an emptiness that they fill with material things and material values. Love needs to fill that gap that void so that each of us can understand the true purpose for our life on earth.

When we come to you we do so in the knowledge that our words will be taken down, will be recorded and used for good. You are sceptical my friend but you will see.

THE UNIVERSE AND MANKIND.

The galaxies are great in their influence, they make the world a brighter and more pleasurable place but in reality they are a myriad of stars and planets. They look beautiful in the sky but each one has its own unique characteristic. They have their own path to travel through the heavens and they affect each other in different ways; in this way or that: One being tied to another and many being reliant upon the single central point. The sun; the moon and the stars all play their part in the grand scheme of things. Each and everyone of them designed as an individual by God from the beginning of time. Blending together yet independent; circling; moving; traversing, each on its own special orbit. Sensing each other but independent; relying upon each other yet separate; looking glorious but in many cases hostile to man's environment. Not uniform nor bland, but special, intricate, problematical and yet important as they express something about God's greatness in the great scheme of things. Repairing and managing; collapsing and being re-born all through the centuries in endless succession; putting forward new shoots; creating new environments, always subscribing to the laws of physics that God had created in the beginning.

Teaching oneself to recognise the uniqueness of the individual is an essential part of growing up, of maturing, of understanding the needs of man. Of penetrating his psyche and seeing that he really is an individual that is learning; growing; experiencing; making mistakes; pulling himself together and moving on: Always as a part of society influencing, sometimes commanding, sometimes being commanded but always part of a pattern of existence like the planets: Going his own sweet way but dependant and influencing others. Coming to their aid in time of need is an essential part of the spiritual agenda, of settling the mind and making it calm. Accepting what is and teaching others to do the same is all without doubt a part of the spiritual. It is the purpose for each and every one of us; the reason for our existence and the very foundation of our need to be needed; to be loved and to love; to help and be helped and even to create and destroy. For change is inevitable as through change we learn. Through moving on we change not only the scenery but our outlook, our minds, our attitudes our whole being. When we look back we recognise the value of the changes, we see that they have brought us great benefit and along with the pain, the suffering the despair and the depression comes a new horizon. Out with the old and in with the new, a way of looking at things which is less cluttered; more simple; more objective; more loving and kind. And we think to ourselves, what a wonderful opportunity that was, an experience which has brought so many riches in its wake. Give yourself a chance, do not lapse into despair but put your best foot forward. All about you there is change, turmoil despair and yet expectation and through these changes many will experience a new dawn; a new revelation and a new understanding of what it is to be human: To be an individual. And the values and the outlook will alter for life is intended to be a training ground, an experience for looking at things in a different way: Making amends; understanding; reaching out; coming to conclusions; and all the while coming closer to God and seeing His face in the people around us. For where would we be without them, imperfect though they are. 31st May 2012

THE TRUE VALUE OF LIFE

Life goes on, people change, and everyone comes to their own conclusion. Love grows in their hearts as they mellow and come to an understanding of the true values of life and when day is done love creates for them a haven, their reward for a life well lived and a job well done. Over the way many voices are calling imploring you to look into your own mind and see the words that are written there. I come to you in peace specialising in the kind of love that is given only to a few. That love which knows no boundaries, which takes no prisoners, which holds no bars, which envelops and intertwines every living soul coming to us like a thief in the night stealing our hearts and minds that we might feel its mighty power growing in each one of us and tending and caring for us as a mother with her children, as a fledgling. And in coming to you tonight we ask that you might be a little more cautious in your expressions that we can come through to you without having to skirmish with your ideas and your words. In truth we come. All about you are radiant beings bringing you their love; their understanding; their hopes for the future; helping you to progress; to blossom and to grow in His image. That you might feel the power of the spiritual that you might understand what it is to be free; that you might take our message to the whole world and help your fellow man to understand. Life is glorious; life is wonderful; life is an opportunity to grow spiritually; to enhance the soul; to enrich it and to bring it great bounties. For in the living of life there are so many things that will furnish the mind with goodness and with opportunities to grow in understanding and in love. Everyone that comes to us will not be disappointed for in your world there are weights and measures, in ours there are circumstances and opportunities and when the one is replaced by the other it brings a greater sense of peace and of harmony and an insight into that which makes us what we are and desires that we go on growing and loving in time that we might keep that spiritual fire burning. Goodnight God bless.

September 2003.

Good evening, everyone is here raising the vibrations and being your good friends and confidants. We read your thoughts we know your mind, we understand your very deep emotions and desires and your fears too. And we come to help you in the name of The Lord. Everyone has a peculiar task to do, we all have our strengths and our weaknesses and so we come to you when you need us. We send the most competent fellow, the person who is able to combat your lower vibrations; your expectations and your anxieties to help you to see the wood for the trees, the light in the gloom and to understand where you are going and how to get there. And though we come unseen and unfelt we are there with great power when it is needed. But you must learn on your own account, you must strengthen your will you must go where you will and learn and understand without our help but we are there when we are called and we help you a great deal: For we are all part of a great body of people who have known each other for centuries. So many times we have interacted with each other, we have had different relationships, mother to father, friend to foe, all kinds of different scenarios that have bound us together in time. And all this to bring us the experience, the knowledge and the understanding of living life as a human being. When the going gets tough we are there to protect you and help you though the hardest times of all are the ones that have the greatest reward. They bring with them waves of glory, of love and friendship which you could never have known if you had not been tested Sometimes we are enemies, sometimes we are friends but all of the time we are learning from each other we are coming together to solve our problems and to help make the world a better place. Without each individual there would be no world, there would be nothing to pit ourselves against nothing to try us to test us to make work harder and so all of these things are sent that we might be better, stronger and greater souls in the world of man and in the world of spirit too. We come to you hoping that you will see brightness in all things, the positive side of life, the things that you get right the things that you do well and the things that you have done for other people and so we bring these thoughts with our great love. Good night and God bless. January2014

WE ARE GREATER BEINGS THAN WE REALISE.
The human being is a definitive being, not all of his thoughts are good not all of them are bad but his limited vocabulary his limited thought patterns are what makes the individual what he or she is. So when you talk of an individual and their

prowess in this or that or their failure to succeed you are talking about a tiny fraction of that real person, the person that you were before you came to earth and the person that you will be when you leave this earth. And so the limits placed upon you by your humanity prevent you from seeing that greater self that more loving and kindly unselfish individual that you really are: Someone that has scaled the dizzy heights and is returning to polish the diamond to make it brighter to succeed where previously he had failed. To understand that frame of mind to know what it feels like and to try to work with it; to coax it; to understand it to challenge it. Whereas the thoughts of the day are limited to the individual as we see him, the person that has grown up in a certain environment and learned all manner of things never-the-less is a tiny, tiny part of the real self, the real you: That which is of God which is magnificent, a being which is so experienced and knowledgeable but which also has the common touch which comes back to live in the world of man to be his child; to be his grandfather; his grandmother; his sister, his husband; or wife and all manner of things: To know what it feels like; to understand the difference; to come to terms with things that we have done which were unwise or cruel or thoughtless; the things which taught us a great deal and lighted the way before us that we may see the contrasts between dark and light between ignorance and understanding between poverty and fortune; love and hate. - So many things; so many conditions; so many issues to come to terms with. You are your own man you like your own way but you are forgiving; you try to understand; you try to make peace with these thoughts and tell yourself that that is their pathway. But we know deep inside the frustrations that you feel when individuals do not follow the path which to you seems obvious but to them not obvious at all as they are distracted by their own thoughts and feelings. Remember this, all of us are greater beings than we realise; all of us are wise beyond our years but all of us too have such a lot to learn: A myriad of experiences, of growth step by step towards the Father in never ending streams we come and we go and we repeat until the light in our lives is so bright, so brilliant that we need not come again.   August 2016.

For those who are interested in the more evidential side of the subject please go to the following.

http://featherstoneblog.blogspot.co.uk/

https://m.facebook.com/mikefeatherstoneartist/?ref=bookmarks

I hope to finish my book 'The Living Dream' in the near future.

Printed in Poland
by Amazon Fulfillment
Poland Sp. z o.o., Wrocław